FUN IN DISNEY WORLD

& THE ORLANDO AREA

1988

Joel A. Glass

FODOR'S TRAVEL PUBLICATIONS, INC.
New York & London

Cover Photo: Len Kaufman/Black Star © 1980

Copyright © 1987 by Fodor's Travel Publications, Inc.

All rights reserved under International and Pan-American Copyright Conventions. Published in the United States by Fodor's Travel Publications, Inc., a subsidiary of Random House, Inc., New York, and simultaneously in Canada by Random House of Canada Limited, Toronto. Distributed by Random House, Inc., New York,

No maps, illustrations, or other portions of this book may be reproduced in any form without written permission from the publisher.

ISBN 0-679-01512-4
ISBN 0-340-42372-2   (Hodder & Stoughton)

Disney World is a registered trademark of the Walt Disney Company.

New titles in the series

Barbados
Jamaica

also available

Acapulco
Bahamas
Las Vegas
London
Maui
Montreal
New Orleans
New York City
Paris
Rio
St. Martin/Sint Maarten
San Francisco
Waikiki

MANUFACTURED IN THE UNITED STATES OF AMERICA
10 9 8 7 6 5 4 3 2 1

Contents

Overview	1
Map of the Orlando Area	9
General Information	10
Where to Stay in the Orlando Area	18
(Excludes Walt Disney World accommodations)	
Map of Orlando Area Hotels, 20–21	
Walt Disney World	39
(Includes accommodations)	
Map of Walt Disney World, 40–41	
Sightseeing Outside Walt Disney World	88
Dining in the Orlando Area	98
Nightlife in the Orlando Area	111
Index	117

Acknowledgment

The author wishes to express his sincere thanks to Jolyn Vargish, without whose patience, understanding, and unequalled research skills this book could never have been done. Thanks go also to Cathy Kerns, whose knack for making sure authors are in the right place at the right time is greatly appreciated, and to the people at hotels, restaurants, attractions, and nightspots whose untiring efforts have gone a long way toward creating *Fodor's Fun in Disney World and the Orlando Area.*

Editors' Note

While every care has been taken to ensure the accuracy of the information contained in this guide, the publishers cannot accept responsibility for any errors which may appear.

All prices quoted in this guide are based on those available to us at the time of writing. In a world of rapid change, however, the possibility of inaccurate or out-of-date information can never be totally eliminated. We trust, therefore, that you will take prices quoted as indicators only, and will double-check to be sure of the latest figures.

Similarly, be sure to check all opening times of museums and galleries. We have found that such times are liable to change without notice, and you could easily make a trip only to find a locked door.

When a hotel closes or a restaurant produces a disappointing meal, let us know, and we will investigate the establishment and the complaint. We are always ready to revise our entries for the following year's edition should the facts warrant it.

Send your letters to the editors of Fodor's Travel Publications, 201 E 50th Street, New York, NY 10022. Continental or British Commonwealth readers may prefer to write to Fodor's Travel Guides, 9-10 Market Place, London W1N 7AG, England.

Overview

Orlando and *fun* have been synonymous since October 1, 1971, when Orlando and, in fact, *all* of Florida, was radically changed forever as *Le Roi Mickey* barreled into the area, bringing with him the largest, most fun-filled attraction ever created for the good-time-seekers of the world.

Virtually single-handedly, Walt Disney World transformed a sleepy, southern, rural, agricultural (some would say redneck) area into a place of national and international attention, interest, and acclaim. Suddenly, the whole world was talking about Orlando,—which is ironic, since Disney World is more than ten miles to the southwest, spanning a massive 28,000 acres and spread over two counties—Orange and Osceola.

Disney World, whose already-strong appeal reached new heights with the October 1982 opening of the futuristic Epcot Center, can, and does, command many days' time to experience completely. Alas, that's one of the more unfortunate sides to this fantastic memorial to one man's incredible vision, for all too many visitors begin and end their stay having seen little of Orlando beyond Disney World.

While the wonderful adventure of the Kingdom of

OVERVIEW   2

the Mouse is well worth a trip to Orlando, limiting oneself to that alone is unfortunate because there is so much more—*worlds* more!—to see and do within a 25-mile radius of Orlando. It is truly a shame not to experience at least some of it.

THINGS TO SEE

First and foremost, of course, are the many sensational man-made attractions. Orlando offers some of the most exciting, enchanting, and diverse attractions in the world.

For instance, not many people know that they can visit the still-rural "Old Florida" Cross Creek area and walk through the home of Marjorie Kinnan Rawlings, author of *The Yearling*, the Pulitzer Prize-winning novel, and many other great books. Another unexplored attraction is the "Bluegrass Country of Florida," that little-known area northwest of Orlando, so called because of its strong resemblance to Kentucky. This hilly area, dotted everywhere with picket fences and horse farms, is rarely seen by outsiders, despite its being famous for the fine stud horses and great racing steeds it has been producing for years. The Orlando area also offers a chance to join a most unusual church service at one of the nation's most important Spiritualist camps in the mysterious community of Cassadaga, where you can have your palm read, your future told, and your "bad vibes" dispelled forever. Park Avenue, in the small but exclusive suburb of Winter Park, is great for browsing, since its shops and boutiques are packed with some of the most beautiful, unusual—and expensive—items this side of California's Rodeo Drive. Winter Park is also home to the Morse Gallery, where you can find the largest collection of original Tiffany art-glass in the world.

The city of Orlando itself was, until a few years ago, a sleepy little town, but it has grown by leaps and bounds as more and more tourists visit and more industry and employees from other parts of the country migrate to what is becoming an increasingly sophisticated city. So, while not really a tourist attraction, as are some cities, Orlando is worth at least a quick look, particularly for its restored historic buildings, its imaginative outdoor murals (such as the colorful 65-foot-long Pine Street wall graphic depicting the history of what was once the city's main street), and that mecca of nonstop fun called Church Street Station, which is credited with creating interest in and development of downtown Orlando.

Both the city and its environs have great natural beauty as well, dotted by more than 2,000 lakes (a few of them man-made), which glisten in the sun as you look down from an arriving airplane.

EAT, DRINK, BE MERRY

One of the more pleasant developments in Orlando has been the burgeoning of its nightlife. When day is done and the blazing red sun is setting, there's still a lot more to stimulate your fancy.

Until a couple of years ago, visitors wanting to eat out had to choose from among the hundreds of fast-food, kiddie-oriented places or the often dreadful and usually overpriced hotel restaurants. But that, too, has changed, and Orlando is currently bursting with interesting places in which to dine on the cuisines of many nations and in many different styles, from formal to laid-back. Even though a few of Orlando's very finest restaurants are in some of the more select hotels, there is no longer any reason why visitors should confine themselves to eating where they're sleeping. To do so is to miss many fine culinary experiences more than capable of holding their own against the offerings of many of the nation's largest, most sophisticated cities.

There's plenty to do after dinner, too . . . if you've got any energy left. One of the worst misconceptions about Orlando is that "there's nothing to do after dark." Until recently, that was largely true, but now it's not. From downtown Orlando to Walt Disney World and the many suburbs, there exists a fine selection of theater, entertainment, concerts, jazz clubs, and discos to suit every taste, whether you are young . . . or young at heart.

Hotels, hotels, hotels

Places to stay can be found everywhere . . . north, east, south, and west of Orlando, and also in the downtown area. They range from extremely inexpensive motels, geared heavily toward families wishing to cook their own meals, to soaring luxury high-rise and chain-affiliated super-structures that are rapidly changing the area's skyline as well as the types of visitors it receives.

So vast has been the recent growth around Orlando that the area now expects to boast more than 61,000 hotel rooms by the end of 1987—more than any city in the United States except New York. By contrast, there were only about 30,000 hotel and motel rooms a scant six years ago.

You can spend as little as $14 or as much as $140 and more per night in places virtually outside the front gates of Walt Disney World or at super-posh, Caribbean-like, full-service resorts. You can be secure in the knowledge that you're minutes away from the Disney attractions, or you can allow the five-mile distance between your hotel and Disney World to feel like light years as you splash in lavish pools and waterfalls after a hot day at the area attractions. You can even stay within the confines of Walt Disney World itself and do away with the worries about commuting daily . . . or several times daily . . . to and from the theme park.

WHEN TO VISIT

The peak vacation periods, and the most crowded times of year in Orlando area hotels and attractions, come around Easter and Labor Day, from late February through April, and in July and August. The week between Christmas and New Year's Day is the busiest week of the year. Not only is *everybody* on vacation, but that's also when the popular Citrus Bowl college football game is played in Orlando.

This means that the absolutely best times to come—if you want a great selection of accommodations, the most economical prices for rooms, and the shortest lines at attractions—are from April through June (except the two weeks surrounding Easter) and from September through early November. The best bargains of all come in September, just after Labor Day, for it's then that most hotels are only about one-third full so their rates are low and the lines at attractions, including Walt Disney World, are almost nonexistent.

Autumn is also part of the rainy season, but let's face it—you can't have *everything*!

When it isn't raining, outdoors enthusiasts who feel they're not getting enough sun and fresh air at the manmade attractions need not despair, for the area hosts more than 30 wonderful golf courses—including three on Walt Disney World property, one at the Grand Cypress Resort, and one at Marriott's sprawling Orlando World Center. Swimming pools, whirlpools, and tennis courts (of which there are more than 750) abound, while several Orlando resorts offer such additional facilities as health spas, jogging tracks, saunas, steam rooms, bicycle rentals, and water-sports equipment.

For Information

There are two places where you can obtain all the information you need to know about Orlando.

The most convenient, once you're in town, is the Orlando/Orange County Convention and Visitors Bureau Information Center, 8445 International Drive, in the Mercado International Plaza just off I-4, near the Orlando Marriott. Open daily from 8 A.M. to 8 P.M. The bureau's main office is at 7680 Republic Drive, Orlando, FL 32819 (345–8882).

The other Orlando information source is the Information Center maintained by the Greater Orlando Chamber of Commerce at 75 Ivanhoe Boulevard in downtown Orlando (425–1234). Hours are Monday through Friday from 8 A.M. to 5:30 P.M. The Chamber Building is on Lake Ivanhoe, just off the Ivanhoe Boulevard exit ramp from I-4.

White Hats

There's one thing you may spot quite often and consider a bit odd about Orlando. Though the city is nearly 60 miles from the nearest ocean, sailors seem to be everywhere, gleaming in their starched white jumpers. No, this is not a case of a ship getting lost; nor is the Navy sailing its fleet on the area's lakes. Orlando is, simply, home to a large U.S. Navy Training Center, which at any given time has an average of 10,500 recruits, and which graduates about 600 new sailors every Friday.

Thumbnail history

Though Orlando wasn't "discovered" until 1971, its modern history dates back to the 1835–42 era, when the area was a campsite for soldiers fighting in the Seminole Indian War.

The story of how the city got its name has been made a bit murky and clouded by the sands of time. There are two theories. One says it came from a soldier named Orlando Reeves who was killed by the Indians while standing guard at the campsite. The other says it's from Orlando Rees, a wealthy plantation owner of the period.

After the Seminole War, not much of note happened until about 1850, when a chap named Aaron Jernigan established a trading post, which was quickly followed by the development and creation, in 1857, of the Village of Orlando. The village's population "soared" to 85 by 1875 but didn't really take off until 1880, when the railroad arrived, permitting large-scale development of a major citrus industry for which the area remains well-known today.

Things were relatively quiet until the 1950s, when the area's population soared by 124 percent, setting the pattern of strong growth that is continuing in the 1980s. A major reason for that growth was the opening of the national space program at Cape Canaveral, just 50 miles east, which induced a large number of high-technology companies, led by Martin-Marietta, to open plants in the Orlando vicinity.

The most recent chapter in the Orlando saga was written in 1971, when the Mouse roared. The rest, of course, is history.

LINES

A word of caution is in order concerning the Orlando attractions, and particularly about Walt Disney World. Try to remember that a *lot* of people want to experience them; Disney World alone receives more than 23 million visitors a year! Because of that, it's inevitable that there are usually going to be long lines, sometimes *very* long lines, at the most popular rides and exhibits. A little strategic timing and a lot of luck may help you avoid much of the crush, and a positive attitude will go a long way in helping you to enjoy your visit.

9   OVERVIEW

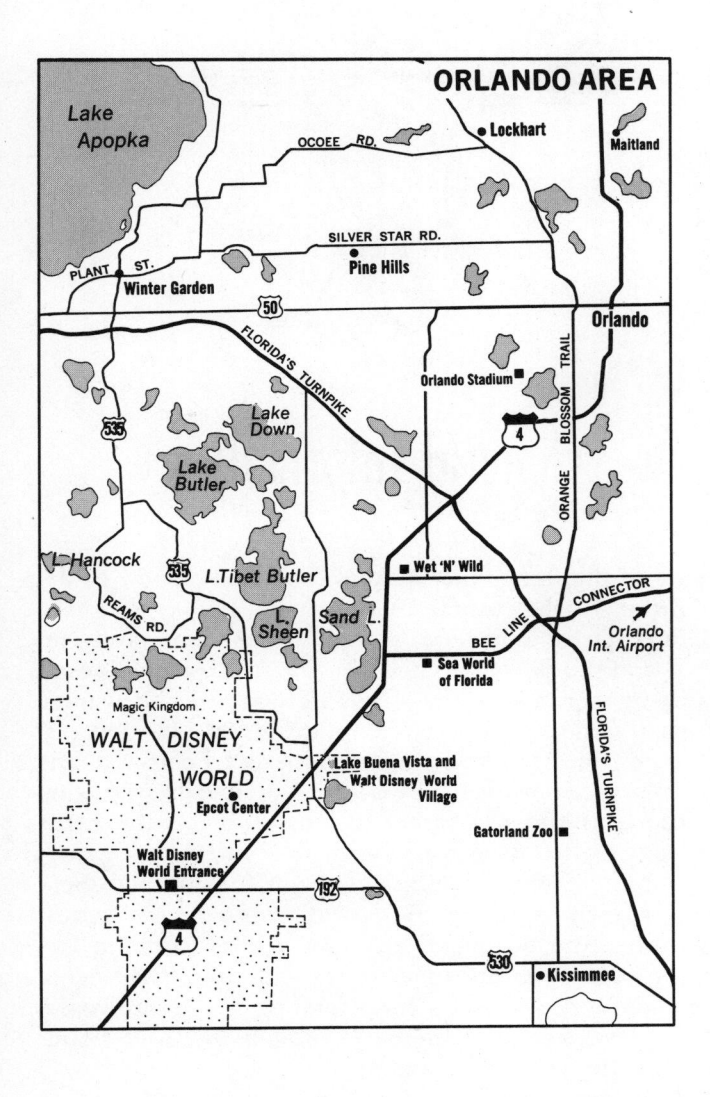

General Information

One of the things that makes a visit to Orlando so delightful is the wonderful weather. Unlike northern climes, Orlando has only two seasons, summer and winter, and the difference between the two usually doesn't vary by more than about 10 or 15 degrees. The average year-round temperature is a delightful 72 degrees, though during midwinter (January and February), the mercury can occasionally scare everyone by plunging close to freezing, a rather unusual and, for the citrus crop, an often disastrous event.

The rainy season extends from July through September, with August and September usually the wettest months. These summer rains most often come in late afternoon so as not to interfere with your sightseeing agenda, and can last for three minutes . . . or three days. You never can be quite sure, though the brief cloudbursts are far more common.

However, there's a good side to this time of the year: the temperature generally cools a bit when rain is nearby (though the humidity soars); nice breezes help keep you cool, and overcast or even slightly rainy days are the best to spend at outdoor attractions because you won't work up the heavy sweat that warm, sunshine-filled days will induce. If you're planning to come to Orlando during this time of year, be sure to bring along an umbrella and/or *light* raingear. These rains can appear without warning, even on an otherwise sunny day, so it is a good idea to keep a small, collapsible umbrella with you wherever you go.

WHAT TO BRING

Generally, during the spring and fall months, the lighter the better; wash-and-wear apparel is especially good because, as you wander about area attractions, you'll find a need to change clothes more often than you do at home. For both men and women, daytime wear for sightseeing should be as light, cool, and comfortable as possible. Shorts for either sex are almost universally accepted daywear in the Orlando area. When they're not, there's sure to be a sign advising you as to the proper attire. Swimgear is very important because you'll want to take a cool, relaxing late-afternoon dip back at your hotel after a day spent at attractions.

Perhaps the four most important items, particularly during summer months, are sunglasses to avoid annoying glare, sunscreen to protect yourself from the semitropical rays, the most comfortable pair of walking shoes you own, and a hat to ward off possible sunstroke. It also wouldn't hurt to bring along some salt tablets in case the long, hot days begin to take their toll by dehydrating your body. (Water fountains at attractions are generally few and far between because the numerous soft-drink concessions don't want to see their business spoiled.)

During winter months the weather can get cool, so bring along a sweater or light jacket. In fact, you may want to have that sweater along during the rest of the year as well since you'll find that many restaurants, hotels, and attraction pavilions feel almost arctic because of the extra-cool air-conditioning. After a long day in the sun, you can become quite uncomfortable if your arms are bare in a cold environment.

For evening wear, slacks and a shirt are acceptable almost everywhere for men; for women, slacks or skirts and a blouse are equally in place. Some of the really fancy restaurants require that gentlemen wear jackets at dinner. Ties, however, are never needed, though some diners, particularly if they're older, often wear them at the more exclusive places.

And, by all means, do not forget your camera and plenty of color film. You're going to be continually motivated to take pictures at the various attractions in the area. While film is readily available in most hotels, attractions, and shops, the price will be higher than at your hometown photo shop.

GETTING THERE

If you haven't flown into Orlando in the last five years, you are in for a pleasant surprise. Gone is the unairconditioned, ramshackle wooden facility that overstayed its welcome since World War II. In its place is an absolutely gorgeous $300 million terminal that opened on September 20, 1981.

Billed as "the Airport of the 21st Century," Orlando International Airport boasts six different concourses with 48 arrival and departure gates. All are connected to the beautifully decorated, futuristic main terminal by the Automated Guideway Transit System, which consists of two elevated 1,950-foot sets of track along which eight people-mover vehicles zip as many as 32,000 passengers an hour. Total time from gate to terminal is less than 90 seconds.

The main terminal, capable of handling 12 million passengers a year, is an aesthetic delight, conceived as a facility that not only makes life easy for travelers but also as one that is environmentally sensitive, with true Florida flair. You *know* you've arrived in Florida once you've stepped into the terminal; the subtropical lakes, streams,

GENERAL INFORMATION

and trees, as well as the interior/exterior landscaping over which stretches a massive glass atrium that allows the sun to bathe the terminal in bright, cheery light, evokes a typically Floridian flavor.

More than 25 scheduled airlines operate to and from the airport, providing direct service to 100 U.S. cities and major points in Canada, Mexico, Europe, and South America.

One of the nicest things about Orlando International is that while it has three levels, all arrivals, departures, baggage pickups, and most ground transportation facilities are laterally placed on the second level, so you usually won't have to travel great distances or up and down stairs and escalators once you arrive.

FOR INFORMATION

If you've got any questions upon arrival, you can get an answer quickly from the information kiosks operated by Walt Disney World and Sea World and from those providing foreign currency exchange and insurance services. All are located in the middle area of the main terminal's second floor.

TELEPHONES

The area code for Disney World and the Orlando area is 305. Dial 800–555–1212, directory information, for toll-free 800 numbers. Charges for local calls from a pay telephone are $.25 in most of the central Florida area. If you make a local call from your hotel room, the charges may be more.

For general information regarding Walt Disney World, call 305–824–4321.

All reservations for hotels or the campground *inside* the Walt Disney World complex can be made through the Central Reservations Office; telephone 305-824-8000.

Emergency Numbers: Within Walt Disney World, for *emergency* ambulance, security, or fire, dial 911 and remain at the telephone until the operator answers and can determine the nature of the call. All Disney World cast members can also help you obtain the right assistance.

TRANSPORTATION

When you've gathered up your bags and are ready to depart for your hotel, you've got a choice between taxi, limousine, bus, or rental car, though a number of area hotels and resorts provide their own van transportation for booked guests. For taxis and limos, the airport has specifically designated official companies, and each has a counter on the second level. Just follow the signs to Ground Transportation.

Cab service operates on a so-called three-tier system under which certain companies are designated "primary," "independent," and "minority." Those nametags really don't mean much to the visitor because the cab companies alternate in picking up travelers at the terminal door on the second level. There's a dispatcher on hand to make sure the business is distributed equally, eliminating some of the pricing shenanigans that take place at many other airports in the country.

The primary cab company is City (Yellow) Cab (422-5151), the independent is Town and Country Cab (828-3035), and the minority company is Ashtin Leasing (851-3812). All are metered—$2.15 at the flag-drop and $1.20 for each additional mile. Average fares to the major resort areas are: Florida Center, $18-$19, Lake Buena Vista, $26-$28, and the U.S. 192 "strip," $33-$40. You should be aware that regulations require cabbies to drop the flag when picking up at the airport, but the meter need not be kept going outside city limits. So if you're heading to places such as Lake Buena Vista, you'll proba-

GENERAL INFORMATION

bly be able to negotiate a flat fare with the driver, if you ask.

If limousines are more your style, your choice is between the primary company, Airport Limo (859–4667), or the minority firm, Beeline Tours (841–1397), both on the second level. Typical one-way, per-person rates are $8 for adults and $4 for children aged four to 14 for trips to Florida Center, and $10 and $5 to Lake Buena Vista or the U.S. 192 area. Cab and limo companies other than the official ones are permitted to operate to and from the airport, but they must use the lower terminal level.

Getting to your hotel by bus from the airport is not a particularly easy job, but it *is* the least expensive way. If you're determined to ride a bus, keep in mind that the vehicles are used for local transportation and thus have very limited space for baggage. Using the bus makes sense only if you're heading for a hotel in the Florida Center area. To get there, pick up Tri-County Transit Authority bus number 11 at the main terminal's Level 1. The bus departs hourly at 20 minutes past the hour, and its ultimate destination is the main terminal in downtown Orlando. There, you need to transfer to the number 8 bus, which travels the length of International Drive, Florida Center's main street, stopping about every block-and-a-half. The total fare will be $.65, including a nickel for the transfer, which you must request when boarding. For bus information, call 841–8240.

TO DRIVE OR NOT TO DRIVE?

The final option for leaving the airport is by rental car. There are two ways of viewing the "do I or don't I?" rental question. You don't really have to rent a car because frequent, convenient transportation is readily available from virtually all hotels to major attractions, and a roundtrip will usually cost you $3 if you're not staying at a resort that's fairly close to the place you wish to visit. On the other hand, since there is no truly convenient public transportation in the Orlando area, and since attractions are very spread out, and taxi fares are high, you simply *must* obtain a car if you want to do anything above and beyond visiting the most major attractions. The cost of renting will likely turn out cheaper than hopping a cab every time you want to go sightseeing, to a show, to dinner, or anywhere else. In common with the rest of Florida, Orlando offers some of the lowest rental-car rates in the entire United States, making it doubly valuable for you to rent. You'll not only save money, but you'll also have the convenience of going where you want, when you want.

Car rental firms with counters on Level 2 of the airport's main terminal are Hertz (800–654–3131), Avis (800–321–1212), Budget (800–527–0700), National (800–328–4567), Dollar (800–421–6868), and Superior (800–237–8106). Rates at companies with offices near, but not actually in, the airport are generally lower. You get to their outlets by stepping outside the terminal and waiting, usually no more than five or 10 minutes, for the various companies' vans to cruise by.

When renting, be sure to take out Collision Damage Waiver (CDW) insurance. It costs a few dollars more, but it's worth it because accidents, particularly on such heavily traveled routes as International Drive and I-4, are more frequent than you might expect.

To rent, you'll generally need to be at least 21 years old (25 if you're a Florida resident) and have a valid driver's license. It's best to use a credit card when paying; otherwise, you'll be forced to post a cash deposit, which can be $50 or more per day.

Getting Around

Because of its rapid growth, Orlando sprawls in every direction, much as Los Angeles does. It's not unusual for people to drive 20 or 30 miles to the many suburban areas in search of good times and fun things to do, so don't let distances get you down; you'll quickly get used to them.

In defining this large area, the most logical geographic breakdowns are downtown Orlando and the Florida Center, Lake Buena Vista, and U.S. 192; all three areas are southwest of the city, en route to Walt Disney World, and house most of the popular and best hotels and resorts. Suburbs with many fine restaurants, shops, night spots, and attractions, such as Winter Park, Maitland, and Altamonte Springs, are located north of Orlando.

THE MAIN DRAG

If you're driving in the area, or plan to, memorize I-4! That interstate not only ties everything together, but whenever you ask directions, you'll invariably receive instructions in relation to I-4, which locals often refer to as "the Expressway."

While it's the area's main high-speed roadway, I-4 is also a bit of an oddity, one which leaves many visitors feeling frustrated and confused. The problem is this: I-4 has been designated an east-west expressway, and it is, if you look at its *total* stretch from Florida's Gulf of Mexico coast on the west to its Atlantic Ocean coast on the east. Where people run into trouble is in the Orlando area, where I-4 actually runs north and south, despite the fact that all Expressway signs are labeled east and west. You'll probably get used to it by the time of your 25th visit to Orlando!

The other main driving headache is Florida Center's International Drive. It's a narrow, winding, two-way street with dozens of partially hidden entranceways, lots of unexpected lane-changes, and, predictably, a good amount of fender-benders. If you want to explore the many attractions, shops, and eating places along this well-known 1.4-mile-long thoroughfare, the smartest thing to do is to park your car at one of the hotels along the strip and walk.

Where to Stay in the Orlando Area

In just the past few years, there has been a vast change in what Orlando has to offer in the way of accommodations. Until recently, the area sprawled with motels of various sizes, offering an assortment of services and amenities; a few were full-service resorts, such as the Orlando Marriott and the Hyatt Orlando, while most of the others were mid-size, often nondescript places good for people staying no more than a night or two.

But a tremendous building boom started nearly four years ago, bringing with it some spectacular new hotels which, in every sense of the word, are world-class resorts, some very fine all-suite hotels sporting rates comparable to those of standard rooms in mid- and upper-priced hotels, and still more chain hotels and motels, many of which are a cut above what those same chains offer in other cities.

A major reason for the fancier new generation of hotels and resorts is that the area, which for many years courted only vacation visitors, suddenly decided to boost the travel trade by offering facilities for meetings and conventions as well as for businessmen and women on sales trips to the many corporations that have been setting up shop in Orlando. This has had good and bad effects. While it has led to an overall upgrading of available accommodations, it also means that during certain times of the year, such as April, May, June, October, and early November, many of those fine hotels are swarming with conventioneers who are often significantly more raucous than the families or couples who flock to the area at the same time. But if you're willing to take a chance on visiting during those periods, you'll also be getting your best breaks on prices, so it's a pretty fair trade-off.

The advent of newer hotels has also brought with it some extremely fine, gourmet restaurants the likes of which had previously existed only outside the hotels.

WHERE THEY ARE

While hotels and motels abound nearly everywhere, the most popular fall into four major groupings—those inside Walt Disney World, those in the adjoining Walt Disney World Village Hotel Plaza at Lake Buena Vista, those in Florida Center/International Drive, and those along the U.S. Highway 192 East and West "strip." If you absolutely and positively must be as close as possible to Walt Disney World but don't wish to pay the cost of being inside it, then the 192 West hotels and motels are for you. But hotels in Lake Buena Vista are only about five or six minutes from the Disney World, and those in Florida Center are only about 15 minutes away, so there's really no need to select your hotel based on its geographic location vis-à-vis Disney or other attractions. Most are convenient to all attractions.

If you don't have a car, every hotel and motel in all three outside-Disney areas is served by frequent transportation to and from the attractions, though the trip will cost you about $3 for the ride on Gray Line of Orlando or Rabbit Lines vans and buses. If you plan to use such

WHERE TO STAY 20

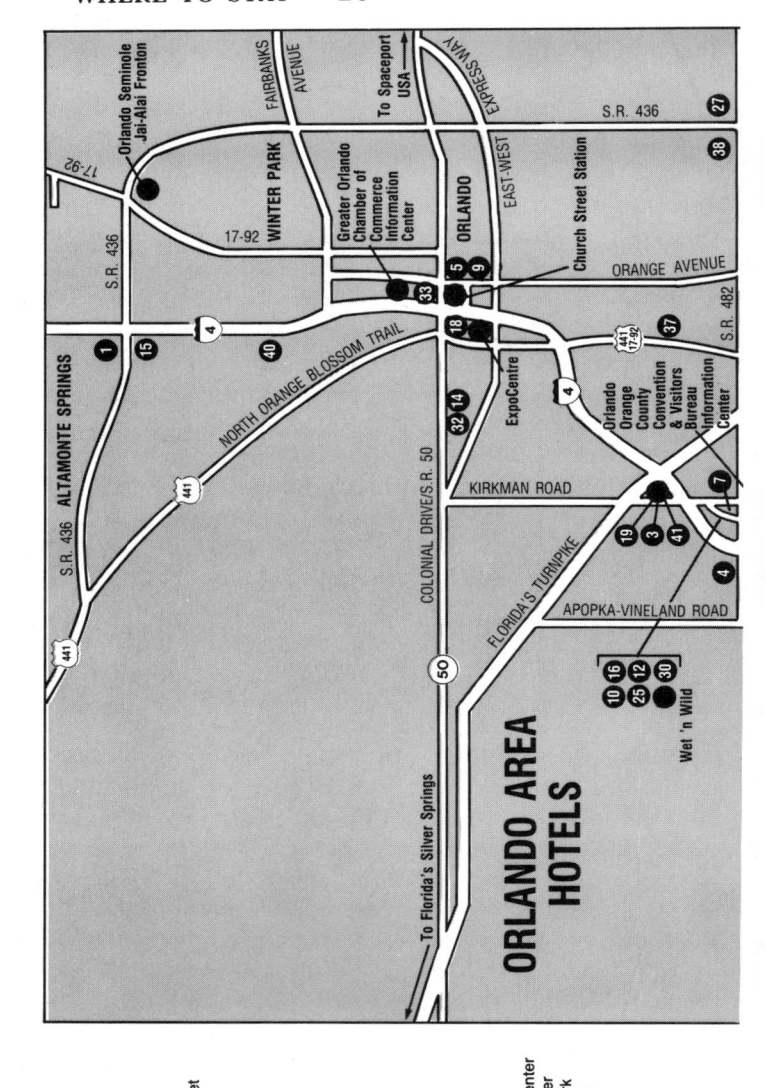

ORLANDO AREA HOTELS

Hotels

1. Altamonte Springs Inn & Racquet Club
2. Buena Vista Palace
3. Court of Flags
4. Days Inn Lakeside
5. Days Inn of America
6. Days Inn West
7. Gateway Inn
8. Grosvenor Resort
9. Harley Hotel
10. Hi-Q Quality Inn
11. Hilton Inn at Disney World
12. Hilton Inn Florida Center
13. Hilton Inn Gateway
14. Hilton Inn Orlando
15. Holiday Inn Orlando Altamonte
16. Holiday Inns Inc.
17. Hotel Royal Plaza
18. Howard Johnson's Executive Center
19. Howard Johnson's Florida Center
20. Howard Johnson's Fountain Park
21. Howard Johnson's International
    Howard Johnson's Lake Buena
22. Vista

21 **WHERE TO STAY**

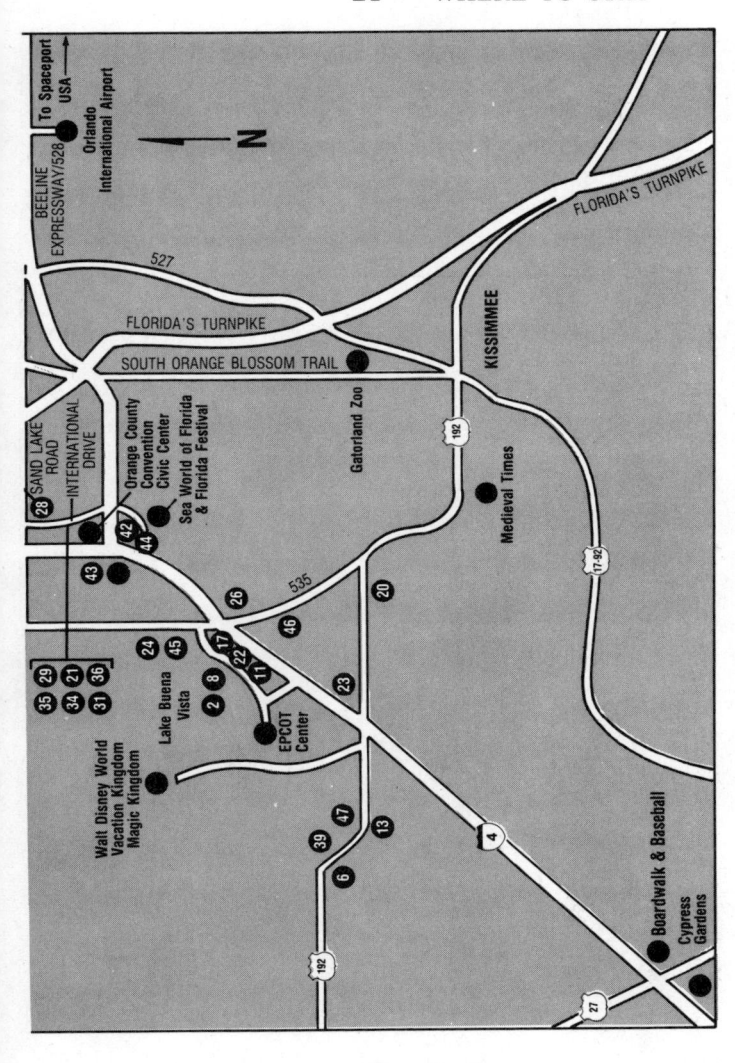

23. Hyatt Orlando
24. Hyatt Regency Grand Cypress
25. Las Palmas Inn
26. Marriott World Center
27. Orlando Airport Marriott
28. Orlando Marriott Inn
29. Orlando Plaza Suite Hotel
30. Quality Inn
31. Quality Inn Plaza
32. Quality Inn West
33. Radisson Hotel
34. Radisson Inn/Justus Aquatic Center
35. Ramada Inn-Plaza International
36. Rodeway Inn International
37. Rodeway Inn (Orlando South Motor Inn)
38. Sheraton Hotel International Airport
39. Sheraton Lakeside Inn
40. Sheraton Maitland Hotel
41. Sheraton Twin Towers
42. Sheraton World
43. Sonesta Village Hotel
44. Stouffer Orlando Resort
45. Viscount Hotel
46. Vistana Resort Inc.
47. Wilson World Hotel Maingate

transportation, check with your hotel desk first because a number of them offer their guests free trips to major attractions. And if you do have a car, a few extra minutes here or there becomes quite irrelevant once you've discovered high-speed I-4.

The inside-Disney hotels, described in the chapter on Walt Disney World, provide the most convenience in terms of seeing the Magic Kingdom or Epcot Center. All you've got to do is check in, leave your car at the hotel, and hop aboard the Disney monorail or bus system to wherever you want to go. But if you want to see or do anything outside Disney property, you've got to get back into your car. Again, trade-offs.

Note: For hotels in this book, all rates quoted, unless otherwise stated, are for one room containing up to two people (with extra charges made for each additional person, in most cases), meals not included. Since some, though not all, hotels change rates several times during the year based on high or low seasons, these changes are explained when applicable. Where no schedule of seasonal rates is listed, it means the quoted prices are valid for the entire year. All rates are subject to change at any time, without notice. Unless otherwise noted, all hotels accept major credit cards, and their telephone numbers are in the 305 area code, though virtually all have national toll-free numbers as well.

TOP-OF-THE-LINE

There are only two hotels in the area that qualify as being in a class of their own, boasting the utmost in luxury, accommodation, services, and facilities. Both are among the newest and, not surprisingly, the most expensive to be found in Orlando. If you seek luxury and resort-like surroundings and are willing to pay for them—and if you don't mind conventioneers—one of these is for you. (Marriott's newer Orlando World Center is priced in the luxury category but because it caters heavily to major conventions, it's difficult to view as a luxury hotel.)

The newest of the top two hostelries, the **Stouffer Orlando Resort,** is also the closest first-class resort to the airport, some 15 minutes away by car. Sitting just across the street from Sea World, the 778-room Stouffer —which opened in December 1984—was the Wyndham Hotel Sea World until late 1986 when it was sold to the Stouffer chain.

The large ten-story hotel can easily be spotted among its flat surroundings as you approach from either I-4, the Beeline Expressway from the airport, or International Drive. Don't be put off by the exterior; swabbed in light beige and topped by a blue roof with two massive, dark-blue, trapezoidal glass skylights and four flag masts, it looks like a Federal office building or, worse, a penitentiary. But once you've stepped inside, you're in for a real surprise. The lobby is a colossal showstopper. With 65,000 square feet, it's longer and wider than a football field and is said to be the largest hotel atrium/lobby in the world. The focal point—placed in the center of the lobby, which is supposed to resemble a European village—is a large, hand-carved Victorian gilded aviary found in Venice, cut into pieces, and transported for reassembly at the hotel. The piece is just one of many antiques and art items to be found around the hotel, all personally selected by millionaire Trammel Crow (whose Dallas real estate company owned Wyndham Hotels) and his wife.

One of the most laudable things about the Stouffer is that its rooms are enormous—20 percent larger than the average hotel room. With the exception of suites, which are even larger, all 718 guest rooms are nearly 390 square feet and elegantly furnished with one king-size or two double beds, carefully selected tropical rattan furniture, decor of either muted pastels or earth tones, good-sized bathrooms with marble touches, and double bathroom sinks.

Room prices are determined by the floor and location. Most expensive are the atrium and outside deluxe rooms on the seventh through ninth floors. (The 10th-level Concierge Floor costs $30 to $40 a night more.) The least-expensive rooms are in the standard category, generally all outside rooms on the fifth through ninth floors and half the rooms on the third and fourth floors. Mid-priced superior rooms face either outside or the atrium, on the fourth through ninth floors. If you want an atrium room but don't want to spend top-dollars for it, request one on the fourth through sixth floors, where rooms are priced the same as superior rooms.

Rates from January through April are $120 for standard, $135 superior, $165 deluxe, and $195 for Concierge Floor. From May 1 through December 14, rates are $105 standard, $115 superior, $135 deluxe, and $195 Concierge Level. Year-round rates for suites range from $300 to $350 for one bedroom and $450 to $585 for two bedrooms.

As if the Stouffer weren't already blessed with virtually everything a guest could want, it's also home to two of the area's finest restaurants, the Continental Atlantis and the gourmet Chinese Haifeng. While the ambience, food, and service are spectacular, so are the prices; nonetheless, both are worth the experience . . . and the money. There are also two moderately priced restaurants in the Wyndham, and two cocktail lounges. Among other facilities are an Oriental art and antiques shop, a bookstore operated by Harcourt, Brace, Jovanovich (which owns Sea World), a health club, Olympic and children's swimming pools, a Jacuzzi, jogging areas, six lighted Omni tennis courts, an 18-hole championship golf course, and a full-service pro shop.

Guests at the Wyndham span the fullest possible range, from businessmen to families on vacation. During peak convention months, the hotel is usually nearly or completely filled with conventioneers.

Stouffer Orlando Resort: 6677 Sea Harbor Drive, Orlando 32831 (351–5555, 800–327–6677).

WHERE TO STAY

The **Hyatt Regency** at Grand Cypress Resort, on the very fringe of—though not actually inside—the Walt Disney World Village Hotel Plaza, opened in January 1984 and is another of that breathtaking new breed of hostelries popping up in Orlando.

The 750-room Hyatt is another landmark, sitting atop a small hill and soaring 18 stories high. Three diagonally attached wings radiate out from the 200-foot-high center atrium of the building. The entire center portion is glass, which not only makes the building stand out from a distance but also brings a light and an airy, tropical feeling into the beautiful atrium lobby, designed to provide a touch of Hawaii.

The pool, a spectacular, tri-level, 800,000-gallon free-form waterway, meanders over nearly half an acre. It passes under rock formations and bridges and also features 12 waterfalls pouring 5,000 gallons of water a minute into the pool; three Jacuzzis; two waterslides, one of which has a 45-foot drop; and a tiny bar hidden inside one of the "caves." Just beyond the pool is 21-acre Lake Windsong, stocked with native Florida fish and boasting a Central Florida rarity—1,000 feet of white-sand beach.

The 7,054-yard, par-72 Jack Nicklaus Signature golf course, designed to resemble a Scottish course, brings tears of joy to the eyes of golfers. The resort's Racquet Club offers 11 tennis and two racquetball courts, where the price to play is $10 an hour.

The Hyatt's rooms, of generous size and decorated with light pastel colors, overhead fans, and live plants, all boast one king-size bed or two doubles, and a small private balcony. The prettiest views are from rooms facing the pool and lake.

Dining facilities include: the casual, fresh seafood-oriented Hemingway's, a Key West-style wooden restaurant perched atop a rock formation overlooking the pool; the formal La Coquina, specializing in nouvelle cuisine that's expensive but nicely served in a beautiful candlelit setting overlooking lush vegetation; the informal Cascade in the lower lobby, which boasts a 35-foot-high sculptured waterfall; and the fast-food Palm Cafe buffeteria on the adjoining patio.

The one drawback to the Hyatt, if you don't like crowds or noise, is that it's one of the most popular convention facilities in the area. The entire super-large lower lobby is devoted to meeting rooms and is frequently packed with convention delegates, as are the main lobby, bars, and restaurants when sessions are over for the day.

Rooms are priced from $150 to $210, depending on floor and view, with those facing the pool or lake from high floors commanding the highest prices. The 11th-floor Regency Club offers much larger, more elaborate, concierge-served rooms at $250, a price tempered just somewhat by the fact that it includes complimentary use of the health club throughout your stay.

Hyatt Regency at Grand Cypress Resort: 1 Grand Cypress Boulevard, Orlando 32819 (239–1234, 800–228–9000).

Lake Buena Vista

Aside from the resorts that are actually inside Walt Disney World, the six that fall within the boundaries of the Walt Disney World Village Hotel Plaza at Lake Buena Vista are the most popular with Disney-goers. There are several reasons for their desirability. They are less than 10 minutes from Walt Disney World, their names are widely known because of management's efforts to promote the hotels, and they are part of an attractive, total complex which includes the popular Walt Disney World Shopping Village as well as several restaurants, lounges, and nighttime showrooms.

There is one slightly confusing thing about the Lake Buena Vista hotels. Even though a lot of people think they are owned by Walt Disney World, they are not. But they are sitting on Disney-owned land and thus pay a percentage of their revenue as homage to the Mouse. In return, Disney keeps a close eye on these hotels to ensure that they maintain certain standards. Technically, only these seven resorts are permitted to say they are in the Lake Buena Vista Village Hotel Plaza, a name owned and jealously protected by the Disney folks.

The seven lucky resorts in the Hotel Plaza are also permitted to identify themselves as "Official Walt Disney World Hotels." That doesn't mean Disney takes full and ultimate responsibility for them, but it does mean that you gain a number of advantages similar to those you'd get by staying at a Disney-owned hotel.

For example, you may book any of the six through the Walt Disney World Central Reservations Office (CRO) by writing to Box 10000, Lake Buena Vista 32830, or calling 824–8000. You're also entitled to many special benefits accorded inside-Disney-hotel guests, such as free rides on the Walt Disney World transportation system. You can also avoid box-office lines at the Magic Kingdom and Epcot Center by buying admission tickets at discounted prices right in your hotel; you can charge food and beverages at Disney World facilities directly to your room; and you can reserve a lunch or dinner spot at the always-in-demand fine restaurants of Epcot Center and the Magic Kingdom in advance by telephone, which no one else can do.

When all rooms are booked at the Disney-owned resorts, CRO personnel will attempt to find space for you at one of the seven "official" hotels unless you direct them not to.

Although Disney World's famed monorail does not go to the Hotel Plaza, you can ride the internal bus transportation system directly to the attraction.

To reach the Hotel Plaza, take I-4 West to the exit for State Road 535, which is clearly marked "Walt Disney World Village." Turn right and at the first stop-light take a left into the Village. You'll be on Hotel Plaza Boulevard, with the resorts before you on both sides of the street.

The finest resort in the Lake Buena Vista Hotel Plaza is the **Hilton,** an 814-room luxury hotel that's a lot prettier inside than out. Its white exterior is a rather staid-looking, 10-story affair composed of three adjoining wings forming a semi-circle around a waterfall, fountain, and palm-lined driveway.

Opened in November 1983, the Hilton caters to meetings and conventions as well as to a large family vacation business, so during certain periods there's quite a bit of hustle and bustle in and around the large number of meeting rooms on the mezzanine level.

One of the hotel's more unusual facilities is its Youth Hotel, a godsend if you're traveling with small children. It has a full-time supervisor and, with its playroom, large-screen television room, and six-bed dormitory, provides a pleasant setting for kids. The Youth Hotel is open daily from 9 A.M. to midnight. It will cost you $4 an hour to obtain some peace, quiet, and the freedom to do what you want to do on your own.

Guest rooms sparkle and glisten as much as the public areas. They're not massive in size, but they are extremely comfortable and nicely decorated. All are the same size, with a choice of king-size or two double beds. Rooms in the front offer a lovely view of the shopping village (the Hilton is the hotel closest to the village), while those in back offer pleasant views of the countryside or pool area.

The Hilton offers one of Orlando's better, most popular, and most luxurious restaurants, American Vineyards, serving New American cuisine; and one of the Benihana of Tokyo steak and seafood chain's newest outlets in Florida. John T's Plantation, off the lobby, is a wonderfully relaxing, people-watching watering hole. There are also a terrace grill and bar, a coffee shop, two lighted tennis courts, two swimming pools and a "spray" pool for children, and a health club.

Rates ranging from $125 to $190 vary by room location and floor, as well as by season, with the higher rates applying to the Christmas through April peak season. The highest-priced rooms are those with a Shopping Village view. However, even if you book a room at the lowest rate, which would be either on a lower front floor or in the back, the check-in clerk will assign you to a better room if one is available, at an extra charge of $30.

Hilton Hotel: 1751 Hotel Plaza Boulevard, Lake Buena Vista 32830 (827–4000, 800–445–8667).

Another one of Orlando's landmarks, the **Buena Vista Palace,** stands out because it soars 27 stories and is built in an unusual triangular shape, sporting a pinkish-beige exterior and an overall look its architect felt resembled a modern high-rise palace. At night, the entire tower appears to sparkle like a procession of heavenly bodies.

Year-round rates are $145 for premium rooms on the eighth through 15th floors; $165 for deluxe on the 16th through 20th floors; and $185 for preferred deluxe on the 20th through 26th floors. The 10th-floor, concierge-serviced Crown Level is priced at $205. A limited number of superior rooms on the first to seventh floors are available for $125.

The hotel's top floor is devoted to the Top of the Palace Lounge, an ideal perch for watching the sun set and Epcot Center's Spaceship Earth's nightly bath in colored lights; and the ultra-exclusive, very formal Arthur's 27 Restaurant, where you'll pay a fixed-price of $52 per person for a seven-course, gourmet Continental meal.

Other facilities include the casual, basement-level Outback Restaurant, featuring beef and huge lobsters served in a surroundings of Australian decor of lots of greenery and a three-story waterfall; the family-style Watercress Cafe, specializing in Florida delights; and the Laughing Kookaburra, an Australian-themed nightclub featuring live entertainment and dancing Monday through Saturday from 5 P.M. to 3 A.M. and a selection of

99 brands of imported and domestic beer. The hotel also has a full-sized, indoor/outdoor, free-form pool as well as a children's pool, poolside lounge and snack bar, four lighted tennis courts, Jacuzzi, and saunas.

Buena Vista Palace: 1900 Lake Buena Vista Drive, Lake Buena Vista 32830 (827–2727, 800–327–2990).

The Buena Vista Palace is owned by the same company as its older neighbor, the **Hotel Royal Plaza,** but there's a world of difference between the two. While the Palace has an air of sophistication and caters to both business travelers and vacationers, the 16-story Royal Plaza is very earthy and quite popular with families that have children along. Both young kids and adolescents seem to enjoy the fun-oriented, extremely casual atmosphere of this place.

The hotel's 397 rooms are well maintained, generous in size, and decorated in pleasant pastels. The most desirable are those overlooking the pool. Rates range from $115 to $160, depending on floor and location. The 16th-floor Crown Level, with concierge service, is priced at $165.

Facilities include three restaurants, two more lounges, poolside cafe and bar, and a putting green.

Hotel Royal Plaza: 1905 Hotel Plaza Boulevard, Lake Buena Vista 32830 (828–2828, 800–327–2906).

The other four Hotel Plaza resorts are the 612-room **Grosvenor Resort,** large, sprawling, and most often used for conventions ($85–$125); the **Viscount Hotel,** 325 rooms in an 18-story tower and a favorite with couples and families ($109–$129); the 323-room **Howard Johnson,** much frequented by younger couples and senior citizens who love its unusual 13-story tropical atrium and upgraded HoJo restaurant in an adjoining building ($135–$165); and the new **Pickett Suite Resort,** the area's only all-suite hotel ($195 single or double).

Grosvenor Resort: 1850 Hotel Plaza Boulevard, Lake Buena Vista 32830 (828–4444, 800–624–4109).

Viscount Hotel: 2000 Hotel Plaza Boulevard, Lake Buena Vista 32830 (828-2424, 800-348-3765).

Howard Johnson's Resort Hotel: 1805 Hotel Plaza Boulevard, Lake Buena Vista 32830 (828-8888, 800-223-9930).

Pickett Suite Resort: 2305 Hotel Plaza Boulevard, Lake Buena Vista 32830 (934-1000, 800-PICKETT).

Near Lake Buena Vista

There are two lovely resorts worthy of consideration that lie just beyond the boundaries of the Lake Buena Vista Village Hotel Plaza.

For tennis buffs, the **Vistana Resort** is nirvana. Sitting on 50 beautifully landscaped acres, Vistana is also popular with couples traveling together and with families because its 314 villa and townhouse units are very spacious, beautifully decorated, and contain all the facilities you've got back home, including fully stocked kitchens.

Vistana provides 14 well-maintained clay and Deco-Turf II courts. There's no charge to play, but racquet rental is from $2 per hour. There are also private and semiprivate lessons available for young and old, amateur and near-pro. A large recreation area opened in 1985 includes a fully equipped exercise room, saunas, steamroom, and, out front, a 250-foot, free-form "super-pool" and kiddie pool.

All units contain two bedrooms. The newest section, called the Spas, features condominiums accommodating up to eight people, while those in the Falls take up to six. The third section, the Courts, contains both townhouses and villas, accommodating six or eight.

When you consider how many can stay in one unit, the rates are among the best bargains in town. From January 4 through February 15 and from May 1 through December 20, prices are $120 to $175, depending on size and location. From February 16 through April 30 and from December 21 through January 3, prices range from $175 to $235.

To get to Vistana, take I-4 West to the State Road 535 exit, turn left and go about three-quarters of a mile. You'll see the entrance on your right.

Vistana Resort: 13800 Vistana Drive, Orlando 32821 (239–3100, 800–327–9152).

When it opened on April 1, 1986, **Marriott's Orlando World Center** boasted more rooms than any place in Florida—1,500 of them. As one of the area's most expensive resorts, and one of its splashiest, it is heavily geared toward the convention crowd.

This Marriott is a deluxe 27-story tower with a 13-story atrium and two attached wings. Included on its 193 acres are a 6,420-yard, par-72 golf course designed by Joe Lee, 13 lakes, 13 unique water features including fountains and waterfalls, 27 elevators, a five-acre activity court out front with more than 1,000 lawn chairs, four indoor and outdoor pools and three hydrotherapy pools, four whirlpools, nine bars and dining rooms including Nikko's Japanese and the expensive, gourmet Regent Court restaurants, and Overtures disco with a marble dance floor and overhead skylights.

Despite the fact that about 75 percent of its business is in meetings and conventions, the Marriott has thoughtfully placed all meeting facilities in a large building that is behind—and separated from—the hotel itself.

Room rates are $145 single and $165 double for golf-course view; $160 and $180 for rooms overlooking the pool/recreation area; and for the Tower rooms which, on the 14th and higher floors, provide magnificent views of the area. Concierge-level rooms are $175, single, $195 double.

To get to the Marriott, drive just past the Vistana Resort on State Road 535 and watch for the hotel's sign on your right.

Marriott's Orlando World Center: 1 World Center Drive, Orlando 32821 (239–4200, 800–228–9290).

THE U.S. 192 AREA

Stretching both west and east from I-4, U.S. 192, in Kissimmee, is a rather uninteresting strip of fast-food restaurants, gas stations, convenience stores, and loads of small and moderately large motels which range from extremely basic to surprisingly nice. These are the places to stay if you want to be as close as possible to Walt Disney World. The many motels along 192, which is also known as Spacecoast Parkway even though the Space Coast is nearly 60 miles away, all cater quite heavily to families and younger couples. Considering how close these motels are to the Disney gates, prices for accommodations along this strip are among the area's most reasonable.

Many of the 192 hotels are affiliated with such well-known chains as Holiday Inn, Howard Johnson, and Ramada Inn, and as such are pretty much the same as you'd find anywhere, though perhaps a bit posher. There are a few that stand out, presenting lovely surroundings along with nice rooms and restaurants.

The **Radisson Inn Maingate,** just minutes from the Magic Kingdom's front door and one of the newest of the strip's hotels, is a 580-room resort.

The hotel has two seven-story wings opening off the lobby. The best rooms are those with a view of the pool. The Radisson's rates of $65 to $95 vary by view and floor. The third floor of the wing, to the right of the front entrance, is devoted to nonsmokers. The oval bathtub in each room is an especially luxurious touch.

Radisson Inn Maingate: 7501 West Spacecoast Parkway, Kissimmee 32741 (396–1400, 800–228–9822).

Lovers of resort-style layouts should head for the nicely done **Sheraton Lakeside Inn,** which offers 652 rooms spread over 25 acres in 15 two-story buildings.

Testimony to its clientele of families and young couples is the strong emphasis on fast-food, and family-style facilities. There are also four lighted tennis courts and an 18-hole miniature golf course.

Room rates run from $60 to $85, depending on view and time of year. The highest rates are from mid-February through mid-April and from mid-June through mid-August.

Sheraton Lakeside Inn: 7711 West Spacecoast Parkway, Kissimmee 32741 (828-8250, 800-325-3535).

Long-time Holiday Inn fans, especially families, head for **Wilson World Maingate** to see what's been created by Kemmons Wilson, founder and former chairman of the Holiday Inn chain. His new, independent endeavor is a somewhat unusual 443-room hotel.

The most striking aspect of this hotel is its 20,000-square-foot, four-story atrium area housing, among other things, a massive heated indoor swimming pool and whirlpool surrounded by palm trees, and a white-tiled lobby floor.

Room rates at Wilson World during the peak seasons (December 16 through April 19 and June 10 through August 23) are $70 single and $75 double. Other times of the year cost $15 less. About 400 of the rooms are classified as standard, meaning there are two queen-size beds and a loveseat. There are also 20 rooms with king-size beds priced at $75 single and $85 double in peak season and $60 and $70 the rest of the year.

Wilson World: 7491 West Spacecoast Parkway, Kissimmee 32741 (396-6000, 800-327-0049).

FLORIDA CENTER

Straddling both sides of I-4, Florida Center actually consists of two portions—the east side of the Expressway, whose main road is International Drive, and the western portion, whose main drag is Major Boulevard.

The original International Drive, the 1.4-mile strip between Kirkman and Sand Lake roads, was built strictly for tourism and is a meandering, curvy, rather dangerous street that's almost always crowded. It's basically a tacky, glitzy strip offering a hodgepodge of fast-food chains, budget-priced family-style restaurants and snack bars, souvenir shops, convenience and liquor stores, gas stations, low-cost hotels and motels, and a few attractions, the best-known of which is Wet 'n Wild.

On the other hand, the opposite portion of Florida Center, across I-4 on Major Boulevard, is a well-maintained, very quiet area that is home to the Sheraton Towers Hotel and Ramada Court of Flags Resort.

Within the past couple of years, International Drive's parameters have been extended with new developments on both ends of the original strip. The southern portion, from Sand Lake Road nearly to Sea World, has become home to some rather classy hotels whose rates are higher than those of the nearby chain properties, and to some rather classy restaurants and night-spots as well as the brand-new Mercado shopping mall. This portion of International Drive is indeed "uptown," devoid of the garish neon signs which predominate on the original part of the street. This part of the Drive is also home to Orlando's pride and joy, the new Orange County Civic/Convention Center, which not only houses large meetings but offers various public performances and concerts as well.

The northern addition to International Drive, extending from Kirkman Road, is being developed as the site of tourist-oriented malls, all offering factory-outlet merchandise.

The biggest hotel "name" on International Drive is the **Peabody Orlando,** opened in the fall of 1986 by the owners of the internationally acclaimed original of the same name that has been operating in Memphis for more than 60 years. The deluxe version in Orlando is 27 stories high, offering 893 rooms and a three-story concierge level on the 25th through 27th floors. Because it's located directly across the street from the Convention/Civic Center, the Peabody is quite heavily oriented to the meetings crowd, from which it gets approximately 80 percent of its business.

Nonetheless, for those who don't object to meshing with conventioneers while on vacation, it's a superb place, reflecting many of the same high standards of personalized service and top-of-the-line food operations that make the venerable Memphis hotel world-famous.

And here's the fun part: if you've ever been to the Memphis Peabody or read about it, you're probably wondering if the famous "parade of ducks" will be repeated in Orlando. The answer is yes. Each day at 11 A.M. and 5 P.M. the string of ducks will waddle across the lobby to and from their very own pool, to the delight of those who are watching. Behind the pool is a 30-foot waterfall, which is the focal point of the four-story tropical atrium lobby.

The Peabody also has six restaurants and lounges, including a very formal and expensive American/Continental gourmet place and a semi-formal Italian one. There are also four lighted tennis courts, a double-Olympic pool that's 150 feet long and 50 feet wide, a children's swimming pool, a full-scale health club, saunas and steam rooms, a licensed day-care center, and a two-mile jogging path winding about the landscaped grounds.

Rates for rooms are based on how high the floor; the concierge-level on top is $175, upper floors are $155, middle ones are $135, and lower floors are $115.

The Peabody: 9801 International Drive, Orlando 32819 (352–4000, 800–262–6688).

The so-called "all-suite" hotels are gaining popularity in Orlando, and the **Park Suite,** which opened its doors in July 1985, is a particularly nice example of the genre. It stands out from its surroundings, eight stories high, boasting a neoclassical facade in light beige.

Rooms at this hotel, which is "home" for a lot of sophisticated business travelers and young couples, are spacious and beautifully decorated in earth tones. All contain a pull-out sofa plus two double beds, a microwave oven, and standup bar with sink for entertaining. The standard-size bathroom is in marble but, curiously, there is a second vanity inside the bedroom.

If you're staying at the Park Suite, you'll also get free breakfast each morning.

Facilities include a restaurant, lobby bar, indoor pool, steam room, saunas, and exercise room. Guest rooms are priced at $95 single and $105 double for the standard one-bedroom suite. The Executive Suite, priced at $110 and $120, is larger and includes a conference table seating six, while the largest Executive Conference Suites have tables seating up to 10 and are priced at $115 and $125.

The Park Suite Hotel: 8978 International Drive, Orlando 32819, (352–1400, 800–822–2323).

The newest addition to this area is about halfway between Florida Center and Sea World—the one-and-a-half-year-old **Sonesta Village Hotel** on Sand Lake, just west of I-4 and less than a mile south of Sand Lake Road.

This is a very thoughtfully and beautifully laid-out "village" indeed, with 369 lavish units in villas spread over 97 acres along the 300-acre Big Sand Lake. This is one of those places that strives to produce a total-resort, typically Floridian feeling and has succeeded. It's heavily oriented toward families, who love the fact that each of the villas contains a full kitchen and everything needed to prepare and consume meals.

There are 20 villas in each V-shaped cluster and all have at least something of a lakeview. They are either one-bedroom units, accommodating up to six, or two-bedroom units, housing up to eight. Each villa has an outdoor sitting area upstairs and private patio at ground level. Accommodations are elegantly appointed in cranberry, blue, and pink, and each boasts original, limited-edition silkscreen prints commissioned by the hotel. All upstairs bedrooms contain two over-sized double beds, and there's also a sleep-sofa downstairs. The two-bedroom units have a second bedroom with queen-size bed downstairs and a loft bedroom upstairs.

Facilities include a restaurant, two tennis courts, eight outdoor hot tubs, and three lakeside beaches (though swimming is discouraged in the natural lake). You can rent Windsurfers for $10 an hour, bicycles for $2 an hour, or parasails for $25 for 10 minutes.

Because of its price, the Sonesta Village Hotel is one of the very best all-around bargains in Orlando. The cost ranges from $110 to $130 for one-bedroom villas and $170 to $210 for two-bedroom ones, depending on the time of year. What you should remember about the Sonesta is that the more in advance you reserve your room, the more likely you are to get a rate at the lowest end of the scale.

Sonesta Village Hotel: 10000 Turkey Lake Road, Orlando 32819 (352–8051, 800–343–7170).

Walt Disney World

You've finally arrived at Walt Disney World. The ultimate in fun . . . the never-ending carnival . . . the land of magic and enchantment . . . the thing that single-handedly put Orlando on the world's map . . . the home of the famed, half-century-old, lovable and adorable Mouse who oversees a lively kingdom indeed. This may be the only place in the world where you can see adults acting like children (in the Magic Kingdom) and children acting like adults (in Epcot Center).

Even if you do nothing else in Orlando, your visit to Walt Disney World will provide a more-than-memorable experience, whether you are eight or 80, because there's something here for everyone and for every taste. The only tinge of sadness comes if you've failed to see and do *everything*, a Herculean task if you're the average visitor to Orlando who stays a mere four days.

Experiencing as much of Walt Disney World as possible calls for serious planning. Since you'll probably be staying only a few short days, you must realize that you cannot see everything. There's simply too much to see. On top of that, remember: while any particular experience at Walt Disney World may last only a few minutes,

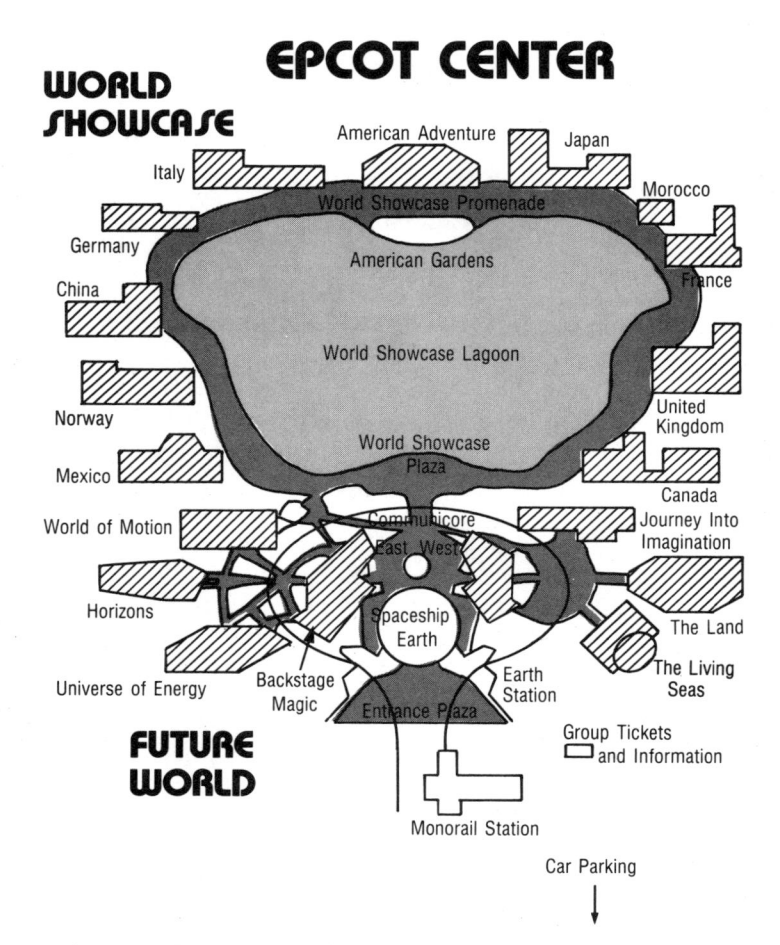

WALT DISNEY WORLD *40*

EPCOT CENTER

WORLD SHOWCASE

- American Adventure
- Japan
- Italy
- Morocco
- World Showcase Promenade
- Germany
- American Gardens
- China
- France
- World Showcase Lagoon
- Norway
- United Kingdom
- Mexico
- World Showcase Plaza
- Canada
- World of Motion
- Communicore East West
- Journey Into Imagination
- Horizons
- Spaceship Earth
- The Land
- Universe of Energy
- Backstage Magic
- Earth Station
- The Living Seas
- Entrance Plaza
- Group Tickets and Information

FUTURE WORLD

Monorail Station

Car Parking ↓

41 WALT DISNEY WORLD

MAGIC KINGDOM

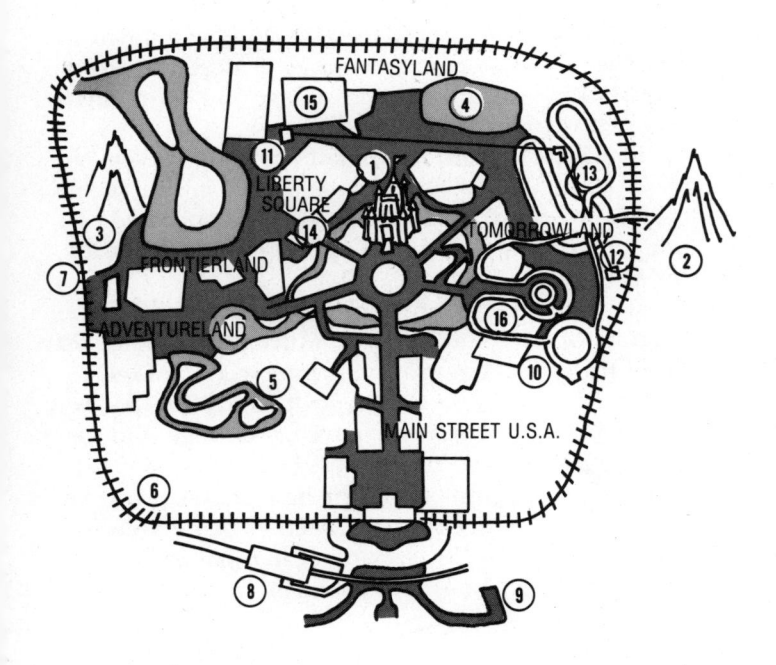

Selected Attractions in the Magic Kingdom

1. Cinderella Castle
2. Space Mountain
3. Big Thunder Mountain
4. 20,000 Leagues Under the Sea
5. Jungle Cruise
6. Walt Disney World Railroad
7. Entrance to Railroad
8. Monorail
9. Ferryboat Landing
10. WEDway PeopleMover
11. Skyway to Tomorrowland
12. Skyway to Fantasyland
13. Grand Prix Raceway
14. Hall of Presidents
15. It's A Small World After All
16. CircleVision 360

during the busiest times of year you may have to wait an hour for the chance at that experience. Lines can be quite long, particularly at the more popular attractions in Disney World.

If you arrive with the idea that you're going to "do" all of Disney, you'll go home disappointed. Instead, try to get to as much as you can of those things that interest you, and keep in mind that you can return, as a very large majority of visitors do. Keep in mind also that repeated visits are not wasted; Walt Disney World is very much an evolutionary endeavor where things change on a continuing basis. There's always *more* to see and do, no matter how many times you come.

It's difficult for the uninitiated to conjure up an image of Walt Disney World because it's layout seems bigger than life and is also somewhat complicated. To realize the enormity of this miracle in Central Florida, consider these facts:

Walt Disney World sprawls over 28,000 acres in the community of Lake Buena Vista, which begins some 20 miles southwest of Orlando, at the intersection of I-4 and U.S. 192. Disney property, much of which has not yet been developed, spans two counties—Orange and Osceola—though most anything that's been developed thus far sits in the "upper" northern half of the property, basically beginning at U.S. 192. Much of Disney World's acreage will never be developed because its master plan calls for retaining thousands of acres in their natural, pristine state for posterity.

Disney World is a self-contained community, with 17,000 to 20,000 employees, its own transportation, vacation, housing, electrical, water, and road systems. It also has its own fire department.

The original attraction at Walt Disney World, the Magic Kingdom, opened on October 1, 1971, on 100 acres — part of an initial 2,500-acre development that also included lakes and golf courses, a campground, and two resort hotels.

Epcot Center, opened on October 1, 1982, fills 260 acres about five miles south of the Magic Kingdom and was designed as a permanent international showplace as well as a display of technological marvels.

More than 200 million people have visited Disney World since its 1971 opening, and attendance each year easily exceeds 20 million. Just to show you how hectic Disney World can get, it has happened more than once that over 125,000 visitors flooded through the admission gates on a single day.

The third major element at Disney World is Walt Disney World Village, which includes seven hotels, hundreds of one-and two-bedroom vacation villas, a public golf club, restaurants, a conference center, an office plaza, nightclubs, and the Walt Disney World Shopping Village.

The Disney hotels

Whether or not to stay in a hotel or resort that is actually within the boundaries of Walt Disney World is a difficult decision to make. The on-site hotels, those owned by the Disney organization and located on the Walt Disney World grounds, offer certain advantages, particularly if the *sole* reason for your visit to Orlando is to experience the Magic Kingdom and/or Epcot Center.

The first factor is convenience.

If you will not have a car during your stay, or even if you will but don't wish to do any unnecessary driving, staying at an on-site hotel solves your major problem. Though none of the on-site hotels is actually within the theme park confines of the Magic Kingdom or Epcot Center, they are very close and, most important, are served by the Walt Disney World internal transportation system. As a guest registered in one of the Disney-owned resorts, that transportation is free.

Note, however, that the well-known elevated monorail serves only two of the on-site hotels—the Contemporary and Polynesian Village Resorts. Staying at one of the other facilities means you'll have to move about on the Disney bus service, which operates frequently, is convenient, and is sometimes faster than the monorail.

Staying on-site, particularly if you're with children,

is an exciting thing to do because it makes you feel as though you're *really* in Disney World. Among the special events offered by the on-site hotels are "character breakfasts" at which full-size Disney cartoon characters appear and charm the kids.

Another advantage is that as a guest of a Walt Disney World resort facility, you'll receive discounts on most of the admission costs to the various theme parks and recreational facilities. Also, rooms at the on-site resorts are among the largest you'll find, generally able to house up to five, because they all were built specifically with families in mind. Another bonus is that the in-room TV sets provide the latest updates on all the special events planned each day and night at Walt Disney World, plus the Disney Channel.

If you're a golfer, three of the finest courses in Central Florida are located inside Disney World. If you're an on-site guest, you'll receive first preference for tee-off reservations. You'll also receive first crack at the always hard-to-get space in most of Disney World's popular fine-dining restaurants, and you'll be able to place the reservations by phone up to two days in advance instead of lining up for them at the attractions.

(Don't, however, overlook the fact that many of the very same benefits are also available to those staying at one of the seven independently owned resorts in the Walt Disney World Village Hotel Plaza.)

Room rates at the on-site hotels are among the highest in the area, a price you must pay for the convenience and fun of staying there. While all Disney resort properties cater very heavily to couples, they are also packed with children, as you'd expect. But if you object to the noise and clutter that hordes of little kids can produce, you'll probably be annoyed quite frequently while staying on-site. Another possible annoyance factor for some is that the best-known on-site hotel, the Contemporary Resort, is a top favorite for large conventions.

Where to stay at Disney World? Options range from Recreational Vehicle campsites to a super-modern highrise hotel, from a resort that will make you swear you're in the middle of the South Seas to one surrounded by beautiful fairways.

WHICH IS WHICH?

The differences between the three major, full-service, on-site resorts are these:

The Contemporary is by far the largest, noisiest, busiest, and most crowded with conventioneers, children, and others, but it's also the absolute center of the action. It has the largest number of in-house dining, entertainment, and shopping facilities of any of the Disney-owned resorts. While many believe the Contemporary is the most popular of the three, for vacationers it's actually the Polynesian Resort that earns that distinction. This place provides much more of a relaxed resort ambience because of its low-rise buildings, exotic, lushly landscaped grounds along the Seven Seas Lagoon, and a paucity of conventioneers. The Disney Inn (formerly called the Golf Resort) is the biggest secret of the three; it's the quietest, most relaxed, and closest to the golf courses. It sits between the Magnolia and Palm courses, and thus is often top-heavy with aficionados of the links, as well as with families. It's also the least-expensive on-site hotel and sports an amiable southern ambience.

If you're with a family or another couple or two and want to try a very different, fun-filled experience, you ought to consider the Resort Villas, of which there are four different types, each with its own particular character. And, for the ultimate in informality, Disney World also provides on-site camping grounds and luxuriously appointed trailers amid the natural woodlands of the lovely Fort Wilderness Resort Area.

BOOKING THEM

All of the on-site facilities may be booked by writing to the Walt Disney World Central Reservation Office, Box 10100, Lake Buena Vista 32830, or by calling 824–8000.

The Contemporary, which is usually at least 96 percent full, can be particularly tough to get a room in, especially during holiday periods or when a lot of conventions are in town. For times like those, most reservations are made 12 to 18 months in advance.

When you contact Central Reservations, if the hotel you're requesting is full the reservationist will recommend and describe alternative on-site resorts. If you don't care for any of them, or if they too are full, you'll be booked into one of the resorts in the nearby Walt Disney World Village Hotel Plaza, unless you indicate otherwise.

Paying up

Bills for hotel rooms, restaurant or entertainment charges, or merchandise purchased anywhere within Walt Disney World may be paid for in cash, by personal check (verified by valid driver's license and major, bank-issued credit card), traveler's checks in U.S.-dollar denominations (or in any denomination if issued by American Express), or with a Visa, MasterCard or American Express credit card. Once you've checked in at your on-site resort, you'll get a guest identification card. This card can be used for free parking at the Magic Kingdom or Epcot Center, to ride the transportation system, or to have bills for food and drink (obtained anywhere on Walt Disney World property except The Magic Kingdom) added directly to your room charges. You can do the same for any merchandise purchased in the Walt Disney World Shopping Village, but not for anything acquired within the Magic Kingdom shops. After your booking for an on-site resort has been processed, you'll receive, by mail, your booking confirmation.

What's New

In 1988, Disney World plans to open the 900-room Grand Floridian Beach Resort, which will sit on 33 acres along Seven Seas Lagoon, near the Polynesian Resort. The hotel's design will be turn-of-the-century Old Florida, and its prices are expected to be the highest of any Disney-owned resort. The monorail system will have a new station at The Grand Floridian, joining those already at the Contemporary and Polynesian Village resorts.

A few other up-and-coming additions to Disney World scheduled to open in 1988 are Pleasure Island, a nightlife and shopping complex consisting of six restaurants and 17 shops; Typhoon Lagoon, a 50-acre water-entertainment center located between the Village and Epcot Center; and the Disney/MGM Studio and Studio Tours, located on 100 acres southwest of Epcot Center. Most of these new attractions will charge a separate admission fee.

The Contemporary Resort

The flagship hotel at Disney World is a massive, 15-story A-frame that looks like a modern concrete version of an ancient Aztec pyramid. In photos and on TV it is usually depicted with a monorail train entering one side and emerging from the other in a tableau that looks not unlike the space shuttle linking up with a satellite station in outer space. With 1,050 rooms, this is Disney's largest hotel; when first built, it represented a tremendous advance in hotel design because it was the largest hotel ever to have used the techniques of modular construction.

The Contemporary is almost as much a show as is Disney World itself. There's always a lot going on and lots of things to do. Check-in for conventions is now on the second floor. This is helping to alleviate a long-existing problem at the Contemporary's first-floor registration desk, where lines were quite lengthy and the wait long at both check-in and check-out, especially if members of a convention were arriving or departing.

Among the resort's most noteworthy dining spots are the gourmet Gulf Coast Room on the second floor and the 15th-floor Top of the World, which offers nightly Broadway entertainment and good food at 6 P.M. and 9:15 P.M. Both places require that men wear jackets, and reservations are mandatory. For the best nighttime view in town of the enchantingly beautiful Magic Kingdom, try the Top of the World Lounge; you'll see a sight you'll never forget. And if you feel a desperate need day or night to escape the razzle-dazzle, noise, and crowds of the Grand Canyon Concourse, try the Outer Rim Lounge for a soothing drink and seafood appetizer.

Rooms at the Contemporary are divided about equally between the Tower and the North and South Garden wings, which surround the pool and lovely gardens. All are large and have private terraces, but those in the wings are priced significantly lower. For many people the latter are the best choice not only because of price but also because they're a lot quieter and removed from the frenetic activity inside the Tower Building. For the best view, request a high floor in the Tower, where rooms are $180. These provide a great vantage point for seeing nighttime fireworks displays over the nearby Magic Kingdom, provided you get a room in the front of the hotel. Rooms in the two wings range from $130 to $160, depending on the view. Most rooms at the Contemporary have two queen-size beds, but those with a king-size bed and sleeper-sofa are available upon request.

Hotel facilities include the Olympiad Health Club on the Tower's third floor. You must take the elevator to get to it because the escalators won't get you there. The club is open Monday through Saturday from 9 A.M. to 1 P.M. for women and 2 P.M. to 6 P.M. for men. You can work out, use the sauna, and shower for $4. Call 824–3410 for information. The Racquet Club has six lighted tennis courts adjacent to the North Garden Wing. The cost is

$6 an hour for singles and $10 for doubles. For court reservations, call 824–3578.

You also can take a motor launch from the hotel to Discovery Island. They leave about every 20 minutes from the Contemporary Marina behind the hotel. Tickets are $6 for adults and $3 for children 3–11. You can buy them in the Tower's main lobby on the fourth floor.

Contemporary Resort Hotel: Box 10000, Lake Buena Vista 32830 (824–1000).

THE POLYNESIAN VILLAGE RESORT

"The Poly," as it's called by insiders, is a delightful full-service resort in a lush, tropical island setting along Seven Seas Lagoon, with the Magic Kingdom clearly visible on the lagoon's far side.

The focal point of this expansive resort is the Great Ceremonial House where you check in. Its atrium center sits high above a large, three-story garden and volcanic rock waterfall surrounded by coconut palms and a wide variety of tropical plants and flowers.

Strung out from the main building are 11 two- and three-story "longhouses," each of which carries the name of a Pacific island, in which the guest rooms are located. All of the resort's suites are in one building—the Bali Hai. Rooms at the Poly have a balcony or patio, except those on the second floor. All offer two queen-size beds and a sleeper-sofa.

If you want to be closest to the main building, with all its dining and entertainment facilities, request a room in the Bora Bora or Maui buildings. For the best view of Seven Seas Lagoon and the Magic Kingdom, head for the Samoa, Moorea, or Tonga buildings.

Room rates are $130 to $150 for garden view, overlooking not only gardens but also the elevated monorail tracks and, across the street, a parking lot; $170 for a somewhat better garden-and-pool-view room, and $195 for rooms overlooking the lagoon. The latter include a host of upgraded amenities and services.

The Poly is Walt Disney World's most popular resort, particularly with families and especially with honeymooners. An astounding 60 percent of its business is made up of people who have been there before, so it must be doing something right.

One thing to keep in mind about this resort is that if you're coming during the rainy season, be sure to have an umbrella. Walking from building to building here means using walkways that are not totally covered.

Polynesian Village Resort: Box 10000, Lake Buena Vista 32830 (824–2000).

THE DISNEY INN

Disney World's third major full-service resort is a wonderful, peaceful place that was once overlooked. The problem had been that its former name, the Golf Resort, had led far too many people to think that if they were not golfers, it was the wrong place for them to stay. The truth is that while the resort is between the Magnolia and Palm golf courses and a number of golfers *do* like to stay here, the place is also a marvelous locale for couples, with or without families, especially if they wish to escape most of the frenzy of activity found at the other resorts.

Rooms at the Disney Inn are large, accommodating at least five, with two queen-size beds and a large sleeper-sofa. The nicest views are from the rooms overlooking its pool. If you book the first floor, you'll be able to stroll easily from your room out to the patio and right onto the pool deck. All rooms are in the North and South Wings, which stretch out from behind the check-in lobby and are attached to it. Rates are $105 for views of woodland, $130 for views of the gardens or fairways, and $140 for pool-view accommodations.

The Disney Inn: Box 10000, Lake Buena Vista 32830 (824–2200).

Playing golf

Just north of the Disney Inn is the 7,190-yard Magnolia Golf Course, while to its south is the 6,967-yard Palm Course, both designed by Joe Lee. Nearby is Disney World's third set of links, the 6,706-yard Lake Buena Vista Course. All are par-72.

The cost of playing at any of the three challenging, 18-hole courses is $50 or, if you're staying at a Disney resort, $40, which includes greens fee and the required cart. There's a special twilight rate of $22 if you're willing to tee off after 3 P.M. There is also a six-hole PGA-sponsored course for beginners called the Wee Links at the Disney Inn. Greens fee for 12 holes of play is $6.30 for juniors up to age 17 and $8.40 for adults.

To reserve a tee-off time, call 824–2270. If you'll be staying at an on-site resort, you may reserve 30 days in advance.

The resort villas

For a totally different type of on-site accommodation, consider staying at one of the Resort Villas, of which there are four different types, each with its own particular character and ambience. These are not quite as plush as the resort accommodations but are ideal for families or couples, particularly those who want to prepare some of their own meals and enjoy being in a non-hotel environment.

Staying at the villas means you're farther away from most things than if you were in one of the three resorts, though Epcot Center is relatively close. In return, you've got a high degree of privacy and a feeling of living in a suburban town, far from the noise, crowds, and freneticism that pervade much of Walt Disney World. If you're a golfer, you'll enjoy staying in the villas because they are the closest accommodations to the Lake Buena Vista

Golf Course. If you're a fishing nut, you'll go crazy over the large bass and other fish to be found in the natural waterways that wend their way through the villas areas. And, for shoppers, the villas are closest to the more than 30 shops and dining facilities comprising the popular Walt Disney World Shopping Village, which is just across Buena Vista Lagoon.

If you opt for one of the villas, you'll probably be happiest by having a car along, though for transportation through the area you can rent a golf cart at a cost of $32 for each 24 hours, and the Walt Disney World bus system can whisk you conveniently to the Magic Kingdom, Epcot Center, and the monorail.

Unlike the full-service on-site resorts, where you can check in at the actual place in which you'll be staying, check-in for all the Resort Villas (except the Club Lake Villas, for which check-in is at the WDW Conference Center) is done at a special Reception Center next to the Viscount Hotel on Hotel Plaza Boulevard in the Walt Disney World Village. At the Center, which is open round-the-clock, you'll be checked-in, given a map to find your way around, and directed to your specific accommodations.

To get to the Reception Center, take I-4 West to the State Road 535/Lake Buena Vista exit, turn right to the first stoplight, then go left onto Hotel Plaza Boulevard and watch for the Center on your right.

THE VACATION VILLAS

These were the first to be built, dating back to 1971. The 133 units here were refurbished during 1986, and the old-fashioned lime-green and yellow decor has given way to more contemporary mauves and beiges. Each unit offers complete living facilities, including kitchen, plus one or two bedrooms. The one-bedroom villas, priced at $150, offer a king-size bed in the bedroom and queen-size sleeper-sofa in the living room. The two-bedroom version, which costs $195, provides a king-size bed or two twins in each bedroom as well as a living room sleeper-sofa.

The Vacation Villas also offer two pools on the grounds.

CLUB LAKE VILLAS

These are the 324 lowest-priced villas, sitting astride Club Lake just north of the Vacation Villas. Built of cedar, these accommodations are the closest to normal hotel rooms, consisting of one bedroom, sleeper-sofa, and wet bar in a total area of about 500 square feet. The reason these villas are smaller—and less expensive—than the others is that they were built not for vacationing families but for those coming to Walt Disney World to attend business meetings at the Walt Disney World Conference Center, which adjoins the northern end of the Club Lake Villas.

Rates for these compact surroundings are $115.

FAIRWAY VILLAS

Sitting northwest of the Vacation Villas and west of Club Lake, these are also built of cedar. The main difference between these 64 units and those at the Club Lake Villas is that the Fairway Villas all have two bedrooms, are considerably more spacious, boast a full loft, and, at $195, are far more expensive. But they are easily the most tasteful looking of all the Resort Villas accommodations, if that's important to you.

The Lake Buena Vista Golf Course is south of the Fairway Villas, but they get their name from the fact that the course's 10th, 11th, 17th, and 18th fairways surround the property on the east, north, west, and south sides, respectively.

Treehouse Villas

A lot of people enjoy staying in these unusual, rather sexy villas, which are the most isolated, sitting on stilts in a peaceful, heavily wooded area. If you really want to get away from it all, this is *the* place. Predictably, honeymooners are just wild about the Treehouse Villas. Even though they are the smallest of the bilevel villas, they are the ones most in demand.

The 60 treehouses, which can make you feel like Tarzan or Sheena when staying in them, all have two bedrooms with queen-size beds and a third bedroom with full-size bed (and so are capable of sleeping up to six), kitchen and breakfast bar, living room, and two bathrooms. The third bedroom and utility room with washer/dryer are on the lower level. The price for this jungle-like experience is $195.

In trying to decide which of the villas is just right for you, remember this: for the least expensive, head for Club Lake; for a unique environment and privacy, the Treehouses; for proximity to the golf course, the Fairways; and for convenience to the Walt Disney World Shopping Village, the Vacation Villas.

Walt Disney World Resort Villas: Box 10000, Lake Buena Vista 32830 (824–6993).

Roughing It

Ardent lovers of the outdoors waste no time thinking about where they're going to stay; they head directly for the Fort Wilderness Resort Area's 730 acres of woodland, streams, small lakes, and water-related activities along the southeastern corner of Bay Lake at the northern edge of Disney World property.

In addition to its camping sites and trailers, Fort Wilderness offers Disney World's premier fun-filled water playground, River Country, with raft rides, rope-swings, and a 260-foot waterslide into the large 330,000-gallon heated swimming pool. In the middle of Bay Lake is Discovery Island, an 11-acre preserve boasting more than 60 species of rare birds and animals, complemented by hundreds of varieties of exotic flowers, plants, and trees. The island is accessible by boat from Fort Wilderness.

Here, in a wonderful sylvan setting, you can rent any of 363 luxurious trailers, of which 289 are 42 feet long, accommodating up to six, and the balance measure 35 feet, taking up to four. Prices are $120 and $100, respectively, including full maid service, so this is not *really* roughing it. Trailer sites, spread over 80 acres, come complete with electrical outlets, outdoor charcoal grill, private picnic table, water, waste container, and sanitary disposal.

Camping sites offer the best opportunity to really rough it on Disney World property and are spread throughout the grounds on 21 separate loops off the main roads. They rent for $25, $30, and $35, depending on location. The highest price is for sites near Bay Lake and its sandy beaches. If you want that location, ask for areas numbered 100 through 500 or 700. For a lower price and denser vegetation, much farther from the lake, book areas numbered 1600 through 1900. (Loops 1500 and 2000 offer the lowest price but lack sewage hookups.) The price for sites may sound high to experienced campers, but when you consider that each site can accommodate up to seven people, they're not bad at all.

Fort Wilderness Resort Area: Box 10000, Lake Buena Vista 32830 (824–2900).

GETTING AROUND

Walt Disney World has a highly developed internal transportation system that can take you anywhere you want to go. Because there is so much territory to cover, it's also a rather confusing system, even to those who have been to Disney World more than once. But remember, Disney World is, in effect, a good-sized "city" and thus requires multiple means of transport able to move thousands of people a day in the most efficient manner possible.

The best-known form of Disney transport is the elevated monorail, which connects both the Magic Kingdom and Epcot Center with the Contemporary and Polynesian Village Resorts. Then there is the extensive bus system, which connects virtually everything. For travel to the Magic Kingdom, there is a ferry system, and there are motor launches linking Discovery Island with Fort Wilderness and the Contemporary. If you're staying at an on-site or Walt Disney World Village Hotel Plaza resort, or you hold a combination Magic Kingdom/Epcot Center ticket, transportation is free. If you're staying elsewhere, free transportation is provided only to specific parks.

MONORAIL

This system operates daily from 7:30 A.M. to 11 P.M., but on days when the Magic Kingdom remains open later than 11 P.M. the monorail continues operating until one hour past that park's closing. The biggest misconception about the monorail system is that it goes *everywhere* in Disney World when, in fact, it serves only the Contemporary and Polynesian Village resorts, the Magic Kingdom, and Epcot Center.

The central connecting station for the monorail is called the Transportation and Ticket Center (TTC). If you are traveling to Epcot Center from monorail stops at the Contemporary and Polynesian Village, you've got to get off at the TTC and connect with the Epcot spur-line. The TTC is also where you can transfer between the Disney bus system and the monorail. Though they're a wonderful way to move about, the monorail trains are often delayed by traffic or mechanical problems, so that while theoretically they should be the most rapid form of travel, sometimes they're not. But they are comfortable and air-conditioned, and if delayed provide an often welcome chance to just sit back and relax.

Bus

The bus system is perhaps most complicated of all. Each bus carries a small color- and/or letter-coded pennant on front and sides. Here's what they signify:

GREEN—Connects the the Disney Inn and Polynesian Village Resort with the TTC. This line operates every 15 minutes from 8 A.M. to 2 A.M.

RED—Connects the TTC, Epcot Center, and Walt Disney World Village. To board one of these buses, you must present a Disney World Resort identification card. This line operates every 20 minutes from 8 A.M. to 2 A.M.

BLUE—Connects Fort Wilderness Resort Area with the TTC. These buses operate every eight minutes from 8 A.M. to 2 A.M.

GREEN and GOLD—If the pennant also has the letters EC or V overprinted, the bus connects all the Resort Villas, Epcot Center, the Lake Buena Vista Club, and the Walt Disney World Shopping Village. If the letters MK are overprinted, the bus connects the villas and the TTC. These lines operate on varying schedules between 8 A.M. and 2 A.M.

SILVER and RED STRIPE—Connects Walt Disney World Village Hotel Plaza and Epcot Center on varying schedules during varying hours. Inquire at your hotel's front desk.

RED and WHITE—Connects the Walt Disney World Village Hotel Plaza with the TTC. This line operates every 20 minutes, from one hour before the Magic Kingdom opens until approximately two hours after it closes.

Motor Launch

This system offers departures about every 20 minutes, and it, too, utilizes color-coded pennants for identification:

BLUE—Connects the Contemporary Resort with the Fort Wilderness Resort Area and Discovery Island between 10 A.M. and 10 P.M.

GREEN—Connects the Magic Kingdom, Fort Wilderness Resort Area, and Discovery Island, but only during hours when the Magic Kingdom is open.

Ferry

There is a ferry service operating across Seven Seas Lagoon connecting the TTC with the Magic Kingdom. It departs from each side of the lagoon about every 12 minutes when the Magic Kingdom is open. It can often get you to the Magic Kingdom quicker than the monorail, which takes the long way around to the front gate. Riding the ferry also gives you a bonus ride that's comfortable, relaxing, and beautiful as it glides over the lagoon's silky waters under clear blue skies. Many people heading for the Magic Kingdom opt for the monorail for the ride there and then take the ferry back at day's end for a chance to relax. If you want to avoid the worst of the lines for both monorail and ferry, take the opposite tack.

Parking

If you arrive at either the Magic Kingdom or Epcot Center by car, there is a $2 charge to park. If you're staying at a Disney World hotel, show your guest ID for free parking. It's very important that you remember precisely where in the parking lot you've left your car because it's easy to lose it in the enormous car disposal area. Frequent trams make stops throughout both attractions' parking areas to bring you to the front gate.

WHEN TO COME

A lot of study has gone into determining the best and worst times to visit Walt Disney World. Of course, it's *always* a great time to come, but "best" and "worst" refer to what are generally thought to be the busiest and least-busy months and days on which to visit.

The absolutely busiest times of all are Christmas through New Year's and the two weeks around Easter, but the time from mid-June through Labor Day, Washington's Birthday week, or Thanksgiving and Memorial Day weekends isn't much better. The best times to avoid the crowds (but remember, even a *slow* time usually means about 20,000 people a day!) is all of January and the first week of February and just after Thanksgiving until the beginning of the Christmas holidays. Almost as slow are the periods from just after Labor Day until Thanksgiving, and from the second week of February to the beginning of Washington's Birthday week.

For most of the year, the busiest days are Monday, Tuesday, and Wednesday. Friday and Sunday are usually the slowest days. Thursday and Saturday are moderately busy. The best time of day to visit is late afternoon and evening (during summer months and holidays when the attractions stay open late). Early morning opening times at the Magic Kingdom and Epcot Center generally draw major crowds, especially during the summer months.

Operating hours at the Magic Kingdom and Epcot Center vary widely throughout the year and also change on days such as legal and school holidays. Generally speaking, however, the longest days are those during prime summer months, when the Magic Kingdom is usually open from 9 A.M. until midnight. During other times of the year, regular hours are from about 9 A.M. to 6 P.M., with Main Street closing one hour later. During Washington's Birthday week, spring school break, Thanksgiving weekend, Christmas holidays, and the two weeks surrounding Easter, the Magic Kingdom remains open later. Epcot Center generally operates from 9 A.M. until 8 P.M., but extends the closing until 10 P.M. or midnight during holiday periods.

To be sure of specific operating hours on any given day, phone 824-4321.

Admission

Visiting Walt Disney World is not a poor man's endeavor, especially if you've got a child or two along, because there is no discounted family admission available. Ticket prices are high, but there is so much to see, do, and experience that you get far more than your money's worth.

There are seven different types of admission tickets, and they all come in two categories—adult, meaning everyone 12 and older, and children aged three to 11. Kids under three get in for free.

The word "ticket" is used by Disney World in only one instance—a single day's admission to either the Magic Kingdom or Epcot Center. The price is $26 for adults and $19.50 for children. If you want to spend two days visiting either or both attractions at Walt Disney World, you've got to buy a separate admission for each day. Beyond that, Disney World has created what it calls the Passport, which admits you to either the Magic Kingdom or Epcot Center or both *on the same day*, along with unlimited use of the internal transportation system.

The Passports, available for three, four, or five days, save you a lot of money and are advisable even if you're staying in the area only for a day or two. That's because each time you use a Passport, the entry date is stamped on it, and then it's returned. You may use up additional days at any point in the future, even years from now. So if you believe there's any chance at all that you'll be coming again, buy—and save—these multiple-day tickets. If you buy a one-day ticket and later change your mind, you can get full credit for it toward the purchase of any Passport by going to City Hall in the Magic Kingdom or to Earth Station at Epcot Center before leaving the park on the day you use it.

Passport prices for adults/children are $70/$53 for three days; $85/$64 for four, and $98/$74 for five days. You also can buy tickets for River Country at $10.75/$8.25 for one day, $16.75/$12.75 for two days, or for Discovery Island at $6/$3. There is a combination River Country/Discovery Island ticket available for $13 adults and $9 children.

One advantage of staying at an on-site hotel or one of the official resorts in the Walt Disney World Village Hotel Plaza is that while you pay the same admission for one-day tickets to the Magic Kingdom, Epcot Center, or Discovery Island, for everything else you get discounted rates for adults/children: three-day Passport, $69/$52, four-day Passport, $83/$62, five-day Passport, $95/$71; River Country/Discovery Island Combination, $12/$8.

Tickets and Passports to both attractions may be purchased at admission booths at the TTC, in on-site or Hotel Plaza resorts (if you're a registered guest), or at the Walt Disney World kiosk on the second floor of the main terminal at Orlando International Airport. If you want to get them before arriving in Orlando, you can send a check or money order for the exact amount to: Admissions, Walt Disney World, Box 10000, Lake Buena Vista 32830. Remember, it usually takes four to six weeks for them to arrive, so order well in advance.

If you wish to leave the Magic Kingdom or Epcot Center, and return on the same day, be sure to have your hand stamped on the way out. You'll need your ticket *and* the hand-stamp to be readmitted.

TOURS

A good way of getting a feel for the layout of either the Magic Kingdom or Epcot Center, along with some interesting commentary about what goes on behind the scenes and inside tips on how to see the attractions in the most logical way, is to take one of the guided tours.

These cost $5 per adult and $3.50 per child on top of the admission price, and usually last three-and-a-half to four hours because they include visits to some of the rides or pavilions. But don't think that taking a tour will get you ahead of any lines; you've still got to wait in place, even though you're with an official tour guide.

The tours depart sporadically, depending on demand. To find out when one may be going, stop at the information desk in City Hall at the Magic Kingdom or Earth Station at Epcot Center, or call 827–8233.

Audio-Animatronics

This mouthful of a word is one you'll see and hear often while at Walt Disney World. It is the name given to a fascinating science, pioneered by the Disney organization, which has produced life-size, realistic-looking figures that surprise you as they begin to move, talk, or sing. You'll be running into Audio-Animatronic figures, which actually are microcomputers dress to look like humans and animals, inside many exhibits at both the Magic Kingdom and Epcot Center.

Getting Assistance

As a quick reference, here are some key telephone numbers you may find handy before or after arriving at Walt Disney World. All are in the 305 area code:
Walt Disney World Information: 824–4321
Magic Kingdom and Epcot Center Tours: 827–8233
Dinner Show Reservations: 824–8000
Walt Disney World Shopping Village Information: 828–3058
KinderCare Child Care: 827–5444

Automobile Service: 824–4813
Resort Guest Activities Information: 824–3737

THE MAGIC KINGDOM

This delight for the young and the young-at-heart was the first of two major attractions built on the Walt Disney World grounds. It offers 45 major "adventures" found in six different "lands" that are spread over 100 acres in a spoke arrangement. Central Plaza is the hub, next to which sits the Magic Kingdom's unmistakable landmark, Cinderella's Castle. In addition to rides and assorted fun experiences, each world is filled with places to eat and shops of all types. The major restaurants and all shops within each land follow the general theme set for the area in which it's been placed.

GETTING THERE

By car, take I-4 West to the clearly marked exit sign for The Magic Kingdom, which will put you onto U.S. 192 West. Exit quickly onto Disney's main entrance road, and follow it for just over four miles to the toll gate. From there it's nearly one mile to the parking areas. If you're staying at the Contemporary or Polynesian Village resort, you can hop aboard the monorail to the TTC station, then transfer to the Magic Kingdom spur-line or to the ferry across Seven Seas Lagoon. From the Disney Inn, take a Green bus; from the Fort Wilderness Resort Area, you'll need either a Blue bus or a Green motor launch; and from the Resort Villas, take a bus with the green and gold MK pennant. If coming from a resort in the Walt Disney World Village Hotel Plaza, take a bus with a red and white pennant.

If you're driving, be prepared for some pretty hefty bumper-to-bumper traffic on I-4 nearing the U.S. 192 exit as well as on 192 itself during the summer and other busy periods. The 12 parking areas at the Magic Kingdom carry Disney cartoon character names such as Donald, Pluto, and Daisy, and every individual parking space within each has its own number. Tractor-drawn trams pass through and stop in the parking areas on a frequent schedule to whisk you to the monorail and ferry to the front gates.

Entering the Kingdom

When you first enter the Magic Kingdom, you'll be in Town Square. If you need any assistance or information, head for the official Information Center inside City Hall on the left-hand side of the square.

A good way to get a feeling for the layout of the Magic Kingdom is to hop aboard the Walt Disney World Railroad, a circular, 1.5-mile ride which takes about 12 minutes to traverse the entire perimeter of the attraction. The only stop is at Frontierland, where you can get off or on. As the train chugs along, you'll be going clockwise from the southern end of the Magic Kingdom, which is where the entrance is, and heading first to its western end, then swinging to the north, east, and back to Town Square. You can board the train in the Victorian-looking station on your right after passing through the front-gate turnstiles.

The four major worlds of the Magic Kingdom are Adventureland in the southwestern quadrant, Frontierland in the western, Fantasyland in the northeastern, and Tomorrowland in the southeastern. Then there is Liberty Square in the northwestern segment and, of course, Main Street, U.S.A., a thoroughfare north of Town Square. Main Street runs to the Central Plaza and is the scene of the wonderful parades of cartoon characters and people staged daily. In a world of its own, jutting out from the eastern boundary of the Magic Kingdom, is the most popular—and scariest—ride of the Magic Kingdom, the circular Space Mountain. You can take advantage of an elevated Swiss-made Skyway connecting Fantasyland with Tomorrowland, if you want to save walking time. Beyond that, it's *à pied* to see all the fun that is available at every turn.

On a truly slow day, such as one in mid-September, it is *possible* to experience just about everything (except shopping) that the Magic Kingdom has to offer because lines are either very short or nonexistent. But don't, if you can help it—the whole point of the Magic Kingdom is to have fun in a relaxed setting, which is missed if you're running around trying to do it all. During busy periods of the year, the best times to enjoy popular attractions of the Magic Kingdom are in the late afternoon or evening.

ADVENTURELAND

In this world, the theme of which is "Adventures in Far-Off Lands," don't miss the **Jungle Cruise,** one of the Magic Kingdom's most popular and enjoyable rides. Unfortunately, it's also one that tends to draw some of the biggest crowds. It only lasts about 10 minutes once you've boarded one of the canopied explorer's launches which follow an underwater track, but it can take an hour or longer on line to reach the boat during the busiest periods.

Once aboard, though, you'll be happy you waited, as the boat wends its way along a "danger-filled" course through the tropical rivers of the world—through a Southeast Asian jungle, the Nile Valley, an African veldt, and an Amazon rain forest. All along the way, you'll pass mechanized animals such as elephants (who squirt water at your boat), lions, vultures, and zebras, as well as cannibals on the "war path." You'll also pass under a drenching waterfall. Throughout the cruise, your boat captain will amuse and delight as he warns about the misadventures faced not only by early "explorers" of this "jungle" but also by some earlier passengers.

The **Pirates of the Caribbean** is a wonderful ride—even better and more fun than the one you may have seen at California's Disneyland. This is a slow cruise through pirate strongholds and treasure rooms populated by Audio-Animatronic figures having a jolly good time as they admire their booty and their women, singing rousing sea chanteys all the while. Even the animals you'll see in the various tableaux are having a good time, as will you.

For some reason lines for Pirates of the Caribbean are usually shorter than for some of the other attractions. So if the ride you want to take looks like a long wait, don't hesitate—head straight for the "Pirates."

Also worth seeing in Adventureland are the **Swiss Family Treehouse,** inspired by the 1960 Walt Disney movie *Swiss Family Robinson,* where you can climb through the home's various levels; and the **Tropical Serenade,** where, inside a Polynesian hut, realistic-looking Tiki birds descend from ceiling perches and talk and sing in several different languages and amuse you with their repertoire of wisecracks and corny jokes.

FRONTIERLAND

Working your way clockwise, you'll arrive next at the world which offers more thrills per capita than any other attraction in the Magic Kingdom. Frontierland's theme is "Colonial History and Frontier Fun," with the emphasis on the latter.

The runaway hit here is the **Big Thunder Mountain Railroad,** which delights shrieking thrill-seekers almost as much as that king of the thrills—Space Mountain. The railroad is one of the Magic Kingdom's newer additions, and one that draws big crowds; luckily, it's worth the wait. If you get queasy, however, you may wish to skip this ride.

For some real cornball fun, pop into the **Country Bear Jamboree** and watch the cast of Audio-Animatronic furry bears sing and joke around in pure down-home fashion. The highlight of this attraction is a "siren" descending on a swing from the ceiling, all wrapped in furs and jewels, enchanting the all-bear cast.

And if that doesn't satisfy your appetite, head for a real Old West show experience at the **Diamond Horseshoe Jamboree,** where good times are the rule. Shows are usually at noon, 1:30 P.M., 3 P.M., 4:30 P.M., and 6 P.M. daily. Before the show begins, sandwiches, snacks, and soft drinks are available. This is a very popular place, and you must make reservations to get in. To book, head immediately for Hospitality House on Main Street, U.S.A., as soon as you enter the Magic Kingdom. Reservations are handed out on a first-come, first-served basis, with the strongest demand usually for the noon and 1:30 P.M. shows.

LIBERTY SQUARE

This small section adjoining Frontierland's southeastern border is made up primarily of Early American-themed shops and eating places, but there are some other interesting attractions as well.

Head first for the **Haunted Mansion,** one of the Magic Kingdom's most imaginative delights. The scene is set as you wander toward the entrance, passing on your left a graveyard with some jocularly inscribed tombstones. Once inside, you enter an eerie elevator, which appears to be descending into the Haunted House's bowels. This attraction is not nearly as scary as it could be, but it presents some fantastic illusions, such as a teapot that pours by itself, seemingly transparent figures floating through the air, and mysterious flying objects nearly everywhere. The tableau of a fully set dinner table for ghosts is absolutely magnificent.

For something a bit more low-key while in this part of the Magic Kingdom, hop aboard one of the **Liberty Square Riverboats,** real paddlewheel steamboats that cross a half-mile track through the Rivers of America, passing along the way a series of reenacted scenes of the Wild West, with human and animal figures and even a log cabin in flames.

The **Hall of Presidents** caused a sensation when it first opened because it was here that Audio-Animatronics was refined. Sitting in this theatrical exhibit is a thrilling experience, as several past Presidents of the United States, at first merely seated and immobile, suddenly begin to move, stand, and relate highlights of the nation's history.

FANTASYLAND

The world in which "Storybook Dreams Come True" is the one most heavily geared toward children, with most of its attractions in the form of basically mild rides. This is also where the well-known **It's A Small World After All**—created for New York's 1964-65 World's Fair—can be found. It's an attraction featuring gaily singing puppets garbed in the native dress of many nations, singing and dancing together in peace and harmony, a favorite theme of the late Walt Disney.

One of the best attractions here is **20,000 Leagues Under the Sea**, a delightful ride inspired by Jules Verne. You descend in a tightly packed submarine, the *Nautilus*, under the command of—who else?—the notorious Captain Nemo, to explore undersea worlds of fantasy and excitement. The submarine doesn't actually plunge underwater, even though it appears to; it merely circles about a lagoon. But in the lower-level compartment from which you peer out through portholes, you'll swear you're at least 20,000 leagues down as you cruise past life-like fish, mermaids, divers, and terrors such as a giant squid and killer fish, pass the lost city of Atlantis, and even cruise under the Arctic icecap.

Peter Pan's Flight is a delight for anyone of any age who's ever read the story of Peter. Seated in a replica of Captain Hook's pirate galleon, you "fly" over a moonlit London toward Never-Never Land to the music of *You Can Fly, You Can Fly*. Accompanying you on the journey are, of course, Tinkerbell, Wendy, and the rest of the characters. The special effects on this ride are just wonderful, particularly the London-by-night portion.

Tomorrowland

Boasting the theme "Fun in the Future," Tomorrowland is, unfortunately, the weakest link of the Magic Kingdom, and thus the one world to skip entirely if time is limited. All too many of the attractions here are oriented heavily toward the commercial interests of their sponsors and, frankly, can be rather boring. The biggest problem is that what originally (in 1971) was truly a look into the future has become "old hat," even to the kids in the late 1980s because they've seen it all on TV or elsewhere.

The best way to decide how much time you want to invest in Tomorrowland is to jump aboard the **WEDway PeopleMover,** where you can rest your feet and relax as the ride works its way throughout Tomorrowland, including peeks into most of its attractions. Sometimes a peek is enough. One glimpse, however, is worthwhile on this trip—the few moments you should take to peer through a tiny section of **Space Mountain,** the most fantastic single element of the Magic Kingdom. If the mountain's darkness, roar of flying roller coaster cars, and the screams of those aboard them aren't enough to scare you out of your wits, then you're probably ready to zip straight to Space Mountain.

Second only to Cinderella's Castle, Space Mountain is a key landmark of the Magic Kingdom, a 180-foot-high, white conical structure that's more than 300 feet in diameter. This ride lasts only about two minutes and 40 seconds, but it can seem like an eternity, if roller coasters scare you, or if you're an old hand at thrill rides. What makes this different from your standard roller coaster, though, is not only that it's indoors but also that it's also quite dark, robbing you of the ability to see what's coming next in the way of sharp drops, a few of which propel the coaster to nearly 40 miles an hour.

Space Mountain is supposed to remind you of a rocketship ride through space, hence the darkness. All around you are wonderful things to see—*if* you're able to keep your eyes open. All the stars and celestial effects you'd expect in outer space are part of this exciting ride, with the darkest—and therefore scariest—portions coming late in the game. The plunges, twists, and turns are sharp and steep enough for you to actually lose things such as a hat or glasses, so be sure you've got all those loose objects carefully stowed away before the ride begins.

And *do* be sure to conquer Space Mountain *before* lunch, not after!

MAGIC KINGDOM DINING

Within the confines of the Magic Kingdom, you'll probably do more snacking or munching than dining. There are no truly great dining experiences here, as there are at Epcot Center, but on the other hand, there's no lack of outlets from which to grab a mouthful or two between attractions. There are more than 30 different places to have anything from a piece of pastry to ice cream, pizza, cookies, chocolate, hamburgers, and hot dogs.

There are four full-fledged restaurants with sit-down service in the Magic Kingdom— King Stefan's Banquet Hall, **Liberty Tree Tavern, Plaza Restaurant,** and Town Square Café. King Stefan's and Liberty Tree require reservations, which must be made directly at the restaurants on the same day you wish to eat in them. They're both popular, so try to book your space as early in the day as possible.

The most enjoyable eating experience is to be had at **King Stefan's Banquet Hall,** which is actually inside Cinderella's Castle and is all decked out in regal decor. Although the waitresses (in typical "castle" garb) try to get you in and out as quickly as possible, the food is surprisingly good, though not always as hot as you might like it. At lunch, served from noon until 3 P.M., there are six entrées available, priced from $5.75 to $8.75. Dinner, served from 4 P.M. until the park closes, offers a choice of four entrées, priced from $15.25 to $18.25. A particularly good choice is the prime rib with Yorkshire pudding. The hot deep-dish apple pie is a wonderful conclusion to your meal.

Lighter fare such as sandwiches, as well as full meals, are served with gusto at the **Town Square Café** on Main Street, U.S.A. Breakfast, available from 8:30 A.M. to 11 A.M., offers standard, hearty, and well-prepared meals priced from $2.50 to $8.50. Lunch features sandwiches from $4.95 to $5.25, and barbecue entrees from $6.95 to $9.95. The barbecue selections at dinner are $6.95 to $12.95. Dessert specialties are priced from $1.95 to $2.50. Children's menus are available.

Epcot Center

After having experienced some of the thrills of the Magic Kingdom such as Space Mountain and the Big Thunder Mountain Railroad, you will find Epcot's rides a lot calmer . . . and indeed they are, for Epcot was designed with a bent more toward adults and precocious children than to the thrill-seeking crowd. Epcot is a subtle blend of the enjoyable and the educational. Its only real problem is that many of its technological marvels were prophetic when first conceived but have become somewhat commonplace now, even though Epcot has only been open a few years.

Getting There

If you're coming by car, take I-4 West to the sign marked Epcot Center. It's about five miles south of the Magic Kingdom exit.

If you're coming from the Contemporary or Polynesian Village resorts, hop the monorail to the TTC station, walk down the ramp, cross to the other ramp, go upstairs and follow signs for the Epcot Line. If you're coming from the Magic Kingdom, take the monorail to the TTC, then cross over to catch the Epcot Line. The 2.5-mile ride from the TTC is the most wonderful way to get to Epcot because the train first loops entirely through Epcot's northern half, providing a splendid overview of all the enchanting things you'll soon be seeing and doing. Kids squeal with delight at their first aerial view of the spectacular Epcot grounds.

From the Disney Inn you can take the bus with a green pennant to the TTC, then transfer to the Epcot monorail. From Fort Wilderness, hop aboard a Blue bus to the TTC. If you're staying at one of the Resort Villas, you'll need to find a bus with the green and gold pennant with the superimposed letters EC. If you're coming from the Walt Disney World Village Hotel Plaza, take one of the buses with a silver and red pennant.

Parking

As at the Magic Kingdom, parking facilities at Epcot Center are extensive, making it easy to forget where you parked if you're not very careful to write down the exact number of the space and the letter of the parking lot in which you parked. Trams circle the parking areas but, unlike those in the Magic Kingdom, these bring you directly to the front gate so there's no need to wait on line for a monorail or ferry to get you to it.

The Layout

Epcot Center is divided almost equally into two distinct areas, separated by the 40-acre World Showcase Lagoon. The northern half, which is where the admission gates are, is filled by Future World pavilions focusing on discoveries and scientific achievements, all sponsored by major American corporations. The southern half is World Showcase which, through the use of pavilions and open-air attractions, gives the feeling that you're taking a grand tour through some of the leading nations of the world. At present, 10 nations are represented, but space already has been allocated for the addition of four more in the near future.

There's a bit of a trick to "doing" Epcot Center. If you want to minimize time spent waiting on lines, do the opposite of what most people do. In the morning, they head for what's closest, and that's Future World. So when you first arrive, avoid that area and make a beeline directly over to World Showcase. In the afternoon, come back and circulate in Future World while most of the crowd has shifted over to where you've already been. Evening hours, of course, are the best for visiting either portion of Epcot.

FUTURE WORLD

The first thing you see when entering Epcot Center is the very symbol of Future World visible from upper floors of hotels as far as 15 miles away—the overpowering, 17-story **Spaceship Earth,** a beautiful silver geosphere perched atop three "legs" that is a sight to behold. At night, it's lighted in several colors, making it appear even more stunning than by day.

The inner-circle of Future World forms a rough triangle, with Spaceship Earth at its apex, Communicore East at the left corner, and Communicore West at the right corner. The outer-circle, beginning left of Spaceship Earth and going clockwise, houses the Universe of Energy, Horizons, and the World of Motion in the eastern quadrant, and, in the western, Journey Into Imagination, The Land, and the Living Seas. The latter, Epcot's newest pavilion (opened January 1986), takes visitors on an "underwater" journey through a saltwater "ocean" that's 203 feet in diameter and 27 feet deep to observe the antics of more than 8,000 sea creatures. High-tech facilities in the pavilion are also being used for marine research projects.

If you're at all interested in having dinner at one of Epcot's many fine and very popular restaurants, the most important place for you to find on entering is Epcot Center Information, situated in the Earth Station building underneath Spaceship Earth. It's here that you must reserve for lunch and dinner and, if you're not there within an hour of Epcot's opening time, you can probably forget about dining at most of the better restaurants that day or night. Booking procedures are detailed more fully in the Epcot Dining section.

Having taken care of your dining reservation needs, it's time to begin enjoying what Epcot has to offer.

Because it's so big, so obvious, and so close to the front gate, AT&T's Spaceship Earth is one of the most popular attractions at Epcot Center, boasting some of its longest lines as well. But regardless of what you do while at Epcot, do not leave before experiencing it.

From tableau through tableau, the ride takes you from the dawn of history through the present, showing major developments in man's methods of communications and intellectual maturity. Spaceship Earth offers some of the most detailed work found anywhere within Walt Disney World. The pity of it all is that the ride moves just a bit too fast for most first-time visitors to fully absorb all that is going on.

Kodak's **Journey Into Imagination** has been an Epcot showstopper since it first opened because of an amazing three-dimensional movie screened in the Magic Eye Theater on the second level of this pavilion. The fanciful 17-minute film starring pop singer Michael Jackson as space traveler Captain EO was done in a new 70 mm process that conveys more realistic images than any other 3-D moviemaking technique ever developed. It's so realistic, in fact, that when costar Fuzzball, a cuddly flying creature, flutters from the screen, he appears to be hanging directly in front of—and just inches away from—*each* member of the audience. Viewers often try reaching out to touch him, and other film objects, which makes watching the audience almost as much fun as watching the film itself. Needless to say, the word has spread about this film and long lines are routine, but showings are continuous and the waits bearable.

The ride in this pavilion is a probe through the realms of imagination, a whimsical 18-minute journey offering a bit of a surprise near the very end. You'll suddenly see a bright strobe light facing you and turning on and off. Actually, your picture is being taken and a few seconds later, just as the ride is about to end, you see a large color photo of yourself displayed on a screen.

If you're just dying for a whiff of what prehistoric life was like, pop into Exxon's **Universe of Energy,** where a ride past a tableau of the Mesozoic Era comes complete with the aroma of the decaying vegetation which led to the formation of oil deposits. A lot of time in this pavilion is devoted to looking at films designed to interest you in the sorts of products produced by its sponsor, making Universe of Energy another bypass entry if your time is limited.

Among the several sideshows at larger pavilions, try not to miss **Kitchen Kabaret** at the Land pavilion, where hostess Bonnie Appetit and a cast of Audio-Animatronic fruits and veggies do their thing in whimsical ways to promote their nutritional values, and the **Bird and the Robot,** tucked into a tiny alcove on the way from the ride to the exit of World of Motion. This is a short but highly imaginative and amusing war-of-wits between a brainy bird and a skilled robotic arm.

WORLD SHOWCASE

The World Showcase concept was for each participating country to instill in visitors a strong sense of what it has to offer those actually journeying there. Obviously, because of the relatively small amount of space allocated for each country, true replicas couldn't be created, but some of the nations have done a splendid job of recreating, on a smaller scale, an example of their best-known features. Thus, France has a replica of the Eiffel Tower, Italy offers a Renaissance-like square,

Morocco has reproduced an authentic Casbah, Mexico, an ancient Mayan temple, and so on.

World Showcase differs from Future World and the Magic Kingdom in that most of its exhibits don't offer rides. The only one that does is Mexico. What World Showcase does offer instead are often breathtakingly beautiful films, exotic national art and cultural exhibits, Audio-Animatronic tableaux, and a host of fine shops and restaurants.

Some of the national pavilions are extremely imaginative and well executed; others, unfortunately, are sorely lacking, making your visit here most enjoyable by picking and choosing.

Some critics have said that some of the pavilions at World Showcase focus far more heavily on shops than on education, entertainment, or fun for visitors. This *is* true in some cases, but many pavilions, while offering some gorgeous items in their shops, also offer wonderful times to be had.

Some of the best fun at World Showcase is not inside the pavilions but in front of them. All, at varying times during the day, put on street shows featuring players in native dress entertaining passersby with comedy, song, dance, and demonstrations of folk arts and crafts.

To reach World Showcase from Future World, walk due south, away from Spaceship Earth, until you reach the lagoon. You'll see the world pavilions stretched out all along the lagoon, and you'll also quickly see just how long a walk it is to circumnavigate that body of water, which is more than one mile around. There are three ways of navigating World Showcase. You can walk from pavilion to pavilion, you can hop aboard one of the rather infrequent, slowmoving double-deck buses that stop in front of every other pavilion, or you can cruise across the lagoon in one of the air-conditioned, 65-foot water taxis. These depart about every 12 minutes. When you first reach the northern shore of the lagoon, you'll see a dock on your left and another on your right. The water taxi leaving from the left-hand dock travels to the Germany pavilion; the one on the right to that of Morocco. Once you've arrived at either stop, you then can walk to adjoining pavilions or hop a bus.

The Pavilions

The centerpoint of World Showcase, sitting directly across the lagoon from the entrance area, is the host pavilion, the American Adventure, which is sponsored by American Express and Coca-Cola. The structures of other countries fan out to the left and right of the American Adventure, forming a large semicircle around the lagoon.

Going in a clockwise direction, starting to the left as you enter World Showcase, are the pavilions of Mexico, the People's Republic of China, Germany, Italy, the American Adventure, Japan, Morocco (the newest, opened in September 1985), France, the United Kingdom, and Canada. Additional pavilions are expected in the near future, beginning with Norway's Gateway to Scandinavia, scheduled to open during 1988.

Perhaps the most exciting pavilion at World Showcase is the entry from the People's Republic of China, a large, red, circular structure that looks like a temple in Beijing. The real crowd pleaser is a magnificent Circle Vision 360-degree film which excellently portrays the beauty, diversity, size, and "faces" of this vast country, including much that has never been seen before by Western eyes. Titled *The Wonders of China,* it surely is that! Because the screens completely encircle the theater, you must stand through this 18-minute presentation, but it's well worth it as you scan the multifaceted country from Mongolia to Beijing, Shanghai to Tibet.

Visitors to the Chinese pavilion flock to this film, making it one of the most popular attractions at Epcot Center, but far fewer stop at the small adjoining structure, which is a shame because that exhibit hall houses absolutely magnificent collections of Chinese artifacts, changed periodically, and really should not be missed. Many objects seen there have never before been outside the People's Republic, and may never be again, so it's a once-in-a-lifetime experience.

The pavilion also includes the Lotus Blossom Café, an open-air, fast-food establishment, and the adjoining Nine Dragons Restaurant, an air-conditioned, sit-down facility offering the cuisines of four regions of the country. Both opened late in 1985.

The American Adventure is one of World Showcase's most popular attractions, particularly with American visitors. The presentation lasts about 30 minutes, and it's a marvelous depiction of U.S. history displayed through stimulating audio-visual effects and some fine Audio-Animatronics figures, such as Ben Franklin and Mark Twain, who discuss the nation's progress through history. Much research went into this sensational performance, which tends to make many Americans burst with pride.

Directly opposite the American Adventure, on the lagoon, is the open-air America Gardens Theatre by the Shore, where live, high-energy all-American shows are performed on an average of four times a day. Show times vary, but are posted each day on boards in front of the theater's entrances.

If you're a fan of beautiful films, see the offering in the China pavilion, and then head for France, which has a well-made film called *Impressions de France,* celebrating the beautiful French countryside to a background of classical music; and then go to Canada, to see the *O, Canada* Circle Vision 360-degree spectacular that zips you from corner to corner of our neighbor to the north.

Several pavilions at World Showcase have one or more particular features that certainly call for a visit. Mexico has reproduced a typical village marketplace where you can pore over and pretend to bargain for items you like; Germany's rollicking Biergarten Restaurant, where food is good, hearty, and inexpensive, is a nonstop carnival with periodic Bavarian shows; Italy's famed L'Originale Alfredo di Roma Ristorante is raucous at night when waiters burst out in arias; the Matsu No Ma cocktail lounge at Japan offers beautiful, relaxing views of the lagoon; and visitors love it when belly dancers start their routines at the Morocco pavilion.

There's always a long line in front of France's popular Boulangerie Pâtisserie, where you can buy some of the finest fresh-baked pastries and croissants you've ever had. The authentically reproduced Rose & Crown Pub in the United Kingdom section draws loads of merrymakers who chat and sip the various ales and beers. Shoppers get extremely excited when they get to the United Kingdom's The Queen's Table and find, in a display cabinet at the rear, the spectacular "Princess Badoura" from the Royal Doulton Prestige Collection, priced at a mere $12,000, and, elsewhere in the shop, "St. George and The Dragon," priced at a "bargain" $7,000.

DINING AT EPCOT

World Showcase offers some of the very finest dining to be found not only at Walt Disney World but in the entire Orlando area. A few of the restaurants have become internationally famous and thus are extremely popular and difficult to book. The top-of-the-line places such as those in the French, Italian, and Mexican pavilions are gourmet with prices that may seem a bit high, but which are lower than what you'd pay in a major city. One nice thing about Epcot's fine restaurants is that they've all got limited-selection children's menus at sharply lower prices, so do what many couples do and bring the kids along.

Because Epcot Center is an all-day sort of experience, it is interesting to note that even for dinner at the very finest, white-gloved gourmet restaurants, diners are permitted to come in very casual dress. Most usually arrive for dinner at the end of a long day spent walking around the various attractions, which makes their men's and ladies' rooms a popular clean-up stop before sitting down to eat. Not having to return to your hotel to change clothes is a great convenience, but it's also something of a shame, because the fine ambience and menus of these restaurants almost cry out for clientele who are dressed as they would be if dining at the same place outside Disney property.

If you want to eat at one of these popular restaurants, you may find it easier to get a booking for lunch rather than dinner; though the overall experience is not quite the same, the prices are lower. And if you're willing to alter your normal eating habits, you'll stand a much better chance of getting a table reservation by having lunch before noon and dinner before 6 P.M. or after 8 P.M.

For dinner, reservations are strongly recommended at L'Originale Alfredo di Roma, Les Chefs de France, Bistro de Paris, the United Kingdom's Rose & Crown Restaurant, The Living Sea's Coral Reef Restaurant, and the San Angel Inn at the Mexican pavilion. They may be necessary at Germany's Biergarten, Japan's Mitsukoshi, and China's Nine Dragons. In most cases, making reservations is a hassle—it's the least-fun part of Epcot Center—but the Disney people have found that there's no way around it, since there are thousands who want to dine in these restaurants each day and only a few hundred who can.

Reservations are accepted on a first-come, first-served system, for both lunch and dinner. Unless you're staying at one of the Walt Disney World resorts, you cannot reserve in advance of the day you wish to eat and you can't book by phone. Instead, you must head for Earth Station, at the base of Spaceship Earth, as soon as you enter Epcot. There you will see a bank of computer screens labeled World Key Information. You need to stand in line to get to one of these screens and place the reservation. Seems pretty simple, but there's a catch: those lines get long and they form early . . . *very* early. On busy days, most available reservations have been gobbled up within an hour after Epcot Center opens. So if you want to be sure of lunch or dinner at one of the gourmet restaurants, you have to line up at the Epcot admissions booth before opening time, and then, when you get through the gate, dash to the World Key computers. Having done that, you can then proceed—casually—with experiencing all that Epcot has to offer.

A service introduced in 1985 permits guests staying

at an on-site Walt Disney World hotel or one of the six in the Walt Disney World Village Hotel Plaza to avoid the reservations race by phoning 828–4000, in advance to secure a dining place for lunch or dinner. Note: if you are staying at one of these resort hotels, you cannot make a same-day reservation. You must book either one or two days in advance, between noon and 9 P.M. When making the reservation, you'll be asked for your name, the name of the resort at which you're staying, and your room number. When you reach the restaurant to honor the reservation, you'll have to show your resort identification card, so don't forget to bring it along.

Epcot restaurants for which on-site and Hotel Plaza guests may reserve in advance are Alfredo's, the Biergarten, Bistro de Paris, Chefs de France, Mitsukoshi, Restaurant Marrakesh, Rose & Crown, San Angel Inn, and, in Future World, The Land Grille Room and Coral Reef Restaurant.

Regardless of how you book, try to show up at your selected restaurant a bit early to be sure of getting your table. Payment for your meal can be in cash, or with American Express, Visa, or MasterCard. If you're a guest at one of the on-site or Hotel Plaza resorts, you may also sign the tab to your room.

THE RESTAURANTS

It's difficult to tell which is more in demand, Les Chefs de France or L'Originale Alfredo di Roma, for many people seem ready to kill to eat in them both. And for good reason—the food is terrific, and so is the atmosphere.

It's a rollicking affair at **Alfredo's** during dinnertime when the waiters skip about singing Italian songs and arias. At lunch, you don't get the musical show, but the jovial Italian waiters joke around with most diners, so it's almost as much fun.

You should consider having fettuccine Alfredo here, since the restaurant was started by the man who invented the dish. In fact, it was this item that made Alfredo De

Lelio famous when he opened his original L'Originale Alfredo in Rome in 1914.

If you don't go for the fettuccine Alfredo, priced at $10.75, try the delicious—and quite filling—*Lo Chef Consiglia,* which means "chef's selection," which consists of a choice of any spaghetti or fettuccine as an appetizer, a mixed green salad, and a choice of any chicken or veal entrée on the six-page menu. This will cost $17.75. Lunch at Alfredo's is less expensive than dinner: entrées are $7.50 to $14.95, while dinner and entrées run from $9.75 to $16.75.

If you're more of a Francophile, head for the French pavilion and take your choice of three dining possibilities, all of which are excellent.

Les Chefs de France is so named because it was created by three of that country's greatest practitioners of gourmet delights: Paul Bocuse, who operates one restaurant north of Lyons and two in Tokyo and has published two best-selling cookbooks; Gaston Lenôtre, who is famed for his pastries and ice creams and runs a pastry school in Paris as well as shops in Paris, Berlin, and Tokyo; and Roger Vergé, who operates a highly regarded restaurant near Cannes on the French Riviera. While none of the three is usually at the restaurant, the chefs who are have been carefully trained to meticulously carry out the masters' instructions.

The restaurant's building has three parts. Aside from Les Chefs de France, there is the **Au Petite Café** adjoining it on the outside and the **Bistro de Paris,** the newest addition, on the second floor above Les Chefs. Entrée prices at the restaurants are $2.95 to $9.95 at lunch and $11.95 to $16.75 for dinner. The difference between them is that Au Petite Café gives you a wide range of choices, from light snacks to more serious fare, while Les Chefs de France offers classic French cuisine and the Bistro specializes in regional cookery from the south of France.

Among the exciting dishes at Les Chefs de France are the roast duck with wine sauce and prunes ($13.95), beef filet with fresh ground pepper, raisins, and Armagnac sauce ($16.75), and filet of grouper topped with salmon and vegetable mousse and baked in puff pastry ($15.75). Upstairs at the Bistro, try one of the regional specialties such as chicken sautéed in pepper, onions, and tomato sauce with rice ($12.50) or the steamed filet of fresh grouper with tomato, mushrooms, fresh herbs, white wine sauce, and rice pilaf ($15.50).

All three restaurants offer a limited, but very fine, selection of French wines, ranging in price from $10.95 to $23 per bottle. You also can order by the glass for $3 to $5.50.

If you're one of the millions who has hopped aboard the gourmet Mexican-fare bandwagon, don't miss the **San Angel Inn** inside the Mexico pavilion, if for no other reason than to cool off and enjoy an absolutely beautiful, almost surreal environment. The Inn is one of those places where you'll probably want to have a light sweater or jacket along because it's kept quite cool.

The San Angel is located between the Mexican crafts market and the "river" along which the pavilion's boat ride cruises. The atmosphere, even during midday, is intimate and romantic because the room is quite dark and there are candles on each table. The best seats, if you can get them, are along the outer rim of the open restaurant opposite the entrance. They are directly above the water, and it's fun to dine while looking at the "river" and watching the boats float by. Seating in this 200-seat restaurant is not terribly comfortable, with tables rather close together and seats of hard-backed, Mexican-style wood. The menu offers a wide selection of tastefully prepared chicken, pork, fish, and beef. Entrées range from $6.25 to $11.50 at lunch, and $8.50 to $16.25 at dinner.

Another enjoyable experience can be found at the **Biergarten,** where it's Oktoberfest year-round. This very popular spot in the Germany pavilion is replete with traditional long communal tables, waitresses in typical Bavarian costume, and the raucous atmosphere one expects to find in a place where yodeling, singing, dancing, and oompahpah bands are heard. The audience, busy quaffing pitchers of German beer or wine and munching on piping-hot pretzels and traditional German food, is usually not at all bashful about joining in the festivities.

Entrées at lunch range from $5.50 for wurst to $7.95 for a pork dish. At dinner, the range is from $9.95 for roast chicken to $26.50 for roast veal shank and dumplings for two, making the **Biergarten** one of the most economical, as well as fun, restaurants in Epcot Center.

Fans of the Oriental food head for the elevated **Mitsukoshi Restaurant** complex at Japan's pavilion. There you've got three choices, but the best is probably the Teppanyaki Dining Rooms, a series of five individual rooms to be found on your left as you enter. Each has four tables seating eight apiece. The focus of each table is a built-in grill on which meats and seafood are prepared in flashy Japanese style, while Kirin beer and hot sake are served to wash it all down. Prices range from $6.95 to $9.75 at lunch, and $11.95 to $19.50 at dinner.

Directly ahead as you enter the complex is the Tempura Kiku, a three-sided counter where you can have a quick meal of batter-fried meats, seafood, and vegetables, with entrées going for $6.95 to $9.75 at lunch, and $11.75 to $17.25 at dinner.

If you're the type who would rather sample a variety of Japanese foods rather than committing yourself to one main dish, go to your right after entering and enjoy a fine view of the lagoon and Spaceship Earth while downing a cold beer or cocktail and a snack of either *Odori* (tempura) shrimp for $4.50, *Kabuki* beef for $3.95, or *Bunraku* chicken for $3.25.

Sensuously gyrating bellies are as much an attraction as the delicious, exotic food at **Restaurant Marrakesh** in the Morocco pavilion. If you've never been to the Middle East or to a Middle Eastern restaurant, stop into this 225-seat establishment and watch the fine belly dancing backed by a three-member Moroccan band, a show which is performed about once every hour during both lunch and dinner. You should also get set for an exciting meal. At lunch, when entrées are priced from $6.95 to $10.95, try the couscous, the Moroccan national dish, served with garden vegetables for $7.50. You can also pick from the wide variety of chicken and lamb dishes, all scrumptiously and authentically prepared. A dinnertime specialty is *bastila,* an appetizer consisting of sweet-and-spicy pork prepared in the Moroccan tradition —layers of thin pastry sheet with chicken strips, almonds, saffron, and cinnamon. Entrée prices range from $7.50 to $14.95.

Finally, try not to miss the **Rose & Crown** in the United Kingdom pavilion. Many visitors, and even Disney employees, gather here for a hearty ale or beer at day's end, or for a fine and reasonably priced lunch or dinner of authentic English pub-grub.

The front room is a replica of a fine old English pub. This is where the drinkers hang out. As in England itself, you're supposed to stand around the bar and "chat-it-up" with your neighbors. There are a few traditional pub tables and chairs opposite the bar, but it's usually all but impossible to find space at them. The dining room is in the rear and beyond it, a lovely outdoor table-and-umbrella set-up features wonderful views of the lagoon and World Showcase.

Waitresses are garbed in English wench outfits and are wonderfully outgoing, even when things get hectic, between about 11:30 A.M. and 2:30 P.M.

Lunch items run from $5.95 for cottage pie to $7.25 for an English mixed grill. Dinner entrées run from $8.25 for fish and chips to $16.50 for a hearty prime rib (with hot-jacket potato instead of the more-usual Yorkshire pudding).

With its excellent, reasonably priced food, and its infectiously cheerful atmosphere, the Rose & Crown is one of the best finds at Epcot Center.

ENTERTAINMENT AT WALT DISNEY WORLD

When it comes to entertainment, there's always a lot going on at Walt Disney World. You never have to leave the immediate environs to enjoy yourself every day and every night. Disney entertainment is often free, such as the Main Street Parade of Disney characters each day at 3 P.M. and the nightly fireworks and laser shows over the World Showcase Lagoon at Epcot Center during the summer months.

More sophisticated nighttime fun is available every night at the **Top of the World** dinner-show in the Contemporary Resort. The rousing Broadway at the Top show runs for about one hour after you've finished dinner and features a group of high-energy performers who sing and dance all-time favorite show tunes. Seating is at 6 P.M. for the 7:45 P.M. show and at 9:15 P.M. for the 11 P.M. show. The price ($35 for age 12 and over, $17 for ages 3–11) includes entertainment fee, choice of appetizer, entré, dessert, two nonalcoholic beverages, and tax. Gratuity and alcoholic beverages are not included.

Jackets are required for gentlemen at Top of the World, a rule that is strictly enforced. Also, because of its great popularity and limited seating space, reservations are necessary. You can—and should—reserve up to 30 days in advance by calling 824–8000.

For those who are left cold by Top of the World's formality and style of entertainment, Disney World has something totally different to offer—the **Polynesian Revue.** To find it, don your casual attire and head for the Polynesian Village Resort's outdoor Luau Cove, where you'll enjoy a beautiful South Seas setting along with some truly well-done island entertainment and a choice of Polynesian dinner dishes served up family-style. Seatings are at 6:45 P.M. and 9:30 P.M., with prices of $23.50 for adults, $19.50 for juniors 12–20, and $14 for those aged 3–11. There's an added feature at 4:30 P.M. daily called "Mickey's Tropical Revue," at which special performances, which absolutely delight children are given by Disney cartoon characters. Prices are $20 for adults, $16 for juniors 12–20, and $10.50 for children aged 3–11.

The height of good old down-home informality and fun comes every evening at the **Hoop-Dee-Doo Revue** at Pioneer Hall in the Fort Wilderness Resort Area. Wiggle into your jeans and brace yourself for some of the world's corniest jokes while downing all-you-can-eat "vittles" of barbecued ribs, fried chicken, corn on the cob, strawberry shortcake, and other goodies. Prices for the nightly sittings at 5 P.M., 7:30 P.M., and 10 P.M. are $25 for adults, $21 for juniors 12–20, and $14 for children aged 3–11.

You can book the Polynesian and Hoop-Dee-Doo Revues even further in advance than the Top of the World shows, and it's a very good idea to do so if you can. If you've booked at an on-site Disney World resort, you can phone 824–8000 to reserve either show as soon as you receive your confirmed reservation number in the mail. If you're going to be staying in the Walt Disney World Village Hotel Plaza, you can call the same number to reserve up to 45 days in advance. If you're staying anywhere else, you can book up to 30 days ahead of time.

Very young kids seem to love the **Character Breakfasts** at which full-size Disney cartoon characters entertain the youngsters for a few hours. The sessions take place each morning from 8 A.M. to 11 A.M. at the Contemporary Resort, 7:45 A.M. to 10:30 A.M. at the Polynesian Village Resort, and 9 A.M. to 10:30 A.M. at the Empress Lilly Riverboat in the Walt Disney World Shopping Village. Prices vary. Advance reservations are required for the Empress Lilly and Polynesian Village breakfasts. Call 824–8000.

Melvin the Moose and Chip 'n' Dale host daily breakfast shows at 8 A.M. and 9:45 A.M. at Pioneer Hall. It's family-style food and fun in an all-you-can-consume mode. Cost is $10 for those 12 and over, $8 for children aged 3–11.

Sightseeing Outside Walt Disney World

As if all that Walt Disney World has to offer were not enough to sate even the most jaded appetite, that famed attraction is in fact just one of many things to do in the Orlando area. Disney World is everybody's number one choice, but within a relatively short drive of Orlando are scores of other manmade and natural attractions, and even some towns and areas that are particularly nice to drive through or explore.

SEA WORLD OF FLORIDA

Sea World is the number two contender for popularity among visitors seeking fun-filled attractions. Located about 10 minutes north of Walt Disney World, it can best be reached by taking I-4 to the Beeline Expressway exit, then going about half a mile to the clearly marked Sea World/International Drive exit, and then to the first traffic light. Make a left turn and, just around the curve in the road, Sea World's entrance will be on the left.

Sea World is a wonderful celebration not only of the seas, but more specifically, of some of the fantastic and lovable creatures that dwell within their realm. The key to this attraction's success is its artful blending of the best elements of an aquarium, a zoological park, and the theater. There are seven major shows and 12 exhibits, all available for a single admission price of $18.95 for adults and $15.95 for children 3–11. Parking is free. The only additional costs are for eating in any of the park's many restaurants and fast-food stands or for taking the spectacular Sky Tower ride to the top of Sea World's landmark, the red-white-and-blue, 400-foot Observation Tower, one of the tallest such structures in the United States. Seating 60 at a time, the observation booth slowly rotates as it climbs to the top, from which flies a massive American flag. The ride, which costs $3 per person, provides a terrific overview of the Sea World grounds as well as of the surrounding area.

During spring, fall, and winter months, Sea World is open from 9 A.M. to 7 P.M. In summer, hours are 8:30 A.M. to 10 P.M.

Sea World of Florida: 7007 Sea World Drive, Orlando 32821 (351–3600).

WET 'N WILD

There's nothing more welcome on a hot, sticky day than splashing about and cooling off. This is where Wet 'n Wild, Orlando's third most popular attraction, comes in handy, for you can not only swim around but can also participate in a number of activities that are exciting and fun for people of all ages.

Situated at the corner of International and Republic drives, Wet 'n Wild has over 14 different water rides, some appealing strictly to children, others to the entire family. You don't even have to know how to swim to enjoy this attraction because water depth never exceeds five feet and there are certified lifeguards always on duty in case you need help.

One of the nice things about Wet 'n Wild is that although it has its fair share of snack stands, it's one of the very few attractions that will allow you to bring in your own food if you wish to picnic around the pool or on the beach.

During most of its operating season, Wet 'n Wild is open from 10 A.M. to 5 P.M. daily. During peak summer periods, from about mid-June through mid-August, hours are extended. The attraction is closed for routine refurbishing from the end of November through mid-February. Admission is $12.95 for adults and $10.95 for children 3–12. Parking is free in an open lot at the corner of Republic Drive.

Wet 'n Wild: 6200 International Drive, Orlando 32819 (351–3200).

South of Orlando

In the areas south and west of Orlando and Walt Disney World are some of the most interesting, fun-filled, and best-known attractions, including one of the oldest in Florida. The easiest way to get to the first group of these is by taking I-4 West to the exit for U.S. 192 East (Spacecoast Parkway) and heading in the direction of Kissimmee. The closer you get to Kissimmee, the more you begin to realize that this is indeed a rural, working cattle and agricultural center as well as the home of several interesting attractions.

GATORLAND ZOO

While in the area you can shift gears to Florida's famed alligators just by continuing about five miles further north on U.S. 441 to Gatorland Zoo, which has one major claim to fame: it's the world's largest alligator farm attraction.

Gatorland is home to about 5,000 alligators and some 30 crocodiles ranging in size from about eight inches to 15 feet. They're spread across a 30-acre park in cages and waterways stretching over half a mile. Adding to the flavor of the place are a number of other animals, birds from around the world, and other specimens of Florida wildlife.

Gatorland's hours from July through September are 8 A.M. to 7 P.M. The rest of the year it is open from 8 A.M. to 6 P.M. Admission is $4.75 for adults and $3.50 for children 3–11. Parking is free.

Gatorland Zoo: 14501 South Orange Blossom Trail, Orlando 32821 (857–3845 for a recording, or 855–5496 for a human).

Two of Florida's best-known attractions are slightly southwest of Walt Disney World, along U.S. 27. To reach that highway, take I-4 West to the U.S. 27 South exit; it's about 18 miles from the Disney World exits.

BOARDWALK AND BASEBALL

The Orlando area's newest attraction sits on property that was formerly home to one of the area's oldest attractions—Circus World. Under its new ownership, the attraction has been expanded to 135 acres and its focus has changed "to combine two great American traditions" —old-time amusement parks, and the national sport, baseball.

Virtually all of the 31 thrill rides that were here during Circus World days remain (18 adult-oriented, 13 child-oriented). Notably missing is the super-charged but somewhat dangerous **Wiener Looping,** now replaced by a 4 1/2-minute flume log ride. Other major rides include **The Hurricane,** one of the country's oldest wooden roller coasters; and the **Zoomerang,** which whips riders around and through high and fast loops. There are also milder diversions, such as a giant Ferris wheel and a traditional carousel.

Nonride attractions include the **Colorado Riders,** an arena show with a 40-member troupe of cowboys and Indians, and the movie **Grand Canyon--Hidden Secrets,** which is shown on a six-story-high indoor screen.

Devotees of the national sport will go bonkers over the six major-league size playing fields, including two stadiums, seating 2,500 and 6,500 respectively. This is the only place in the world where you can watch a baseball game virtually any day of the year.

During the February–April spring training season, the Kansas City Royals play here (beginning 1988); in summer months, a local Florida State League Class A team holds sway. In between, the stadiums are filled with high-school and college games along with tournaments and games played by the park's own Central Florida League team.

The park is open daily from 9 A.M. to 10 P.M. till midnight Friday and Saturday). Admission is $16.95 for adults, $12.95 for children measuring 48 inches or less in height. If you only want to see a baseball game, admission is $2.50 (higher when the Royals are playing).

Boardwalk and Baseball: Box 800, Orlando 32802 (648–5151).

CYPRESS GARDENS

Lovers of great natural beauty served up with fun and excitement always make a point of stopping at Central Florida's oldest continuing attraction. This is a place where you'll hate yourself for not bringing a camera because it is one of the most breathtakingly beautiful attraction in the entire state, if not the entire country.

Cypress Gardens, opened on January 2, 1936, sprawls over 223 of the most meticulously landscaped acres you've ever seen, along the shores of Lake Eloise. Despite the fact that it's been around for over 50 years, the attraction is as popular, exciting, and beautiful today as it was on opening day when it filled just 16 acres of former swampland.

Cypress Gardens has more than 8,000 thriving exotic plants and flowers which bloom year-round, helped along by a staff of 53 horticulturalists. Depending on the season, you're likely to see tropical and subtropical plants, trees and vines, giant cascading bougainvillea, delicate orchids, bursting roses, fragrant gardenias, iridescent flame vines, and thousands more. Flora and fauna have been drawn from more than 70 countries for this garden, which includes such rare specimens as shell ginger from China, Jatroha from Nigeria, water lillies from New Zealand, and lollipops from Peru.

To get to Cypress Gardens, which is about 30 miles from Walt Disney World, take I-4 West to the U.S. 27 South exit. Follow signs for Winter Haven. When you reach Waverly, watch for State Road 540 on your right, turn onto it, and drive about three miles to the gardens' entrance.

Hours are 9 A.M. to 7 P.M. daily, though these are extended on certain peak days. Admission is $14.95 for adults, $9.95 for children 3–11.

Cypress Gardens: Box 1, Cypress Gardens 33880 (813–324–2111, 800–237–4826).

SIGHTSEEING

If you've seen all the attractions that interest you and would like to get a feel for the Orlando/Central Florida area, there are a number of other interesting things to see and do, all within a relatively short drive of the major hotel areas.

ORLANDO

For starters, you might want to get an idea of what the actual city of Orlando is all about. While it's still relatively small, Orlando has been growing and changing rapidly in recent years as more and more businesses move in, triggering construction of high-rise office buildings and radically altering the look of the downtown area. More importantly, Orlando is a city with an interesting history and some wonderful old buildings to be admired. Many of these buildings and surrounding streets have been refurbished and once again look as they did many, many years ago. There are also some nice outdoor murals to be seen.

The best way of seeing the city is to take one of the guided walking tours conducted by the Junior League. These focus on Orlando's history and its architecturally significant buildings. The one-hour tours are free and begin each Thursday morning at 10 A.M., except on holidays, from the kiosk in Wall Street Plaza, at the corner of Orange Avenue and Wall Street. For information, phone the Junior League's administrative office between 9 A.M. and 2 P.M., Monday through Friday, at 843-7463.

Wine Country

A well-kept secret is that the Sunshine State is also a wine-producing state. Modest production, granted, and modest wine, too, but it's here nonetheless. There are three wineries in Florida that actually maintain their own vineyards and two others that produce wine by utilizing other growers' grapes.

The only full-scale winery in Central Florida is at the delightful little Florida Heritage Vineyards just outside the tiny town of Anthony. To get there, take the I-75 to State Road 326 exit and head east to U.S. 301. Take a left (heading north) and go to N.W. 114th Street, then turn right at the Heritage sign. When you hit Magnolia Street, turn right to the winery.

Florida Heritage Vineyards and Winery: Box 116, Anthony 32617 (904-732-3427).

Old Country

For most people Central Florida didn't exist until Walt Disney World opened in 1971, but the area actually has quite a bit of history that dates back to well before the Mighty Mouse arrived.

The tiny town of Micanopy is on the National Register of Historic Places, claiming to be the oldest town in inland Florida not on a waterway. It's also a town that "made it" in Hollywood by being used for street scenes in the popular movie about author Marjorie Kinnan Rawlings, *Cross Creek*.

In 1821 a brave soul named Edward Wanton moved into the ancient Indian village of Cuscowilla to establish a trading post. As the town grew slowly, it was often referred to as "Wanton's Town," but the name was later changed to Micanopy in honor of the great chief of that name who headed the Seminole Indian Nation. During the Seminole Wars of 1835-42 there was a major fort here, but it was burned and left no remains. Today, the most interesting part of this colorful town is its Historic District, which has no less than 39 buildings and sites of historic interest packed into an area of just a few blocks.

There are many beautiful two-story homes, most with porches in the Victorian style, surrounded by well-maintained gardens and tree-shaded streets. The oldest part of town is along both its main street, Cholokka Boulevard, an ancient Indian trading path, and Ocala Street, which intersects the foot of Cholokka. On Ocala once stood the old fort and original trading post. Just stroll around, take pictures, and enjoy yourself.

Micanopy is somewhat tricky to find because it's slightly off the beaten path. To locate it, take I-75 North and exit at Irvine (State Road 320 East). When you reach U.S. 441, take a left onto 441 North and go to County Road 25-A, which will be a left-hand turn. About half a mile up that road you'll run straight into Cholokka Boulevard and Micanopy's Historic District.

The millions of people who grew up on the Pulitzer Prize-winning novel about rural Florida, *The Yearling*, never leave this part of the state without stopping in at the home of its famed author, **Marjorie Kinnan Rawlings,** who lived there from 1928 until her death in 1953. She's buried in a small cemetery nearly eight miles east of the home.

The rambling, cracker-style Rawlings home, which sits on a 72-acre farm along Orange Lake, dates back to the early 1800s. It is now a State Historic Site and, as such, has rangers on hand to lead you through the various parts of the old home while explaining the author's life and times.

The home is open Thursday through Monday from 9 A.M. to 11:30 A.M., and from 1 P.M. to 4:30 P.M. Guided tours, which cost $.50 per person for anyone older than 6, begin every half-hour. Parking is free.

To find the site, take U.S. 441 to State Road 346, almost one mile south of the Micanopy turnoff. Go east on 346 to State Road 325 and turn right directly to the home, which you'll spot on the right-hand side.

Marjorie Kinnan Rawlings State Historic Site: Route 3, Box 92, Hawthorne 32640 (904–466–3672).

SPIRIT COUNTRY

For a really *different* excursion in another area of Central Florida, head for **Cassadaga,** home of one of the nation's largest communities for psychics. Visiting the Cassadaga Spiritualist Camp is, if you've got an open mind, a fascinating experience, because psychics and other members of the Spiritualist Church live and work here, and they welcome visitors who wish either to sit in on one of the unusual church services or to visit with any of the mediums, spiritualists, or psychic healers who are part of the camp.

The Cassadaga Spiritualist Camp is about 35 miles northeast of Orlando. To get there, take I-4 East to Exit 54 for Lake Helen and Cassadaga. Follow County Road 472 to the intersection with County Road 4139, take a right and follow the road until you reach the camp, easily spotted by its sign on the roadway's right-hand side.

Cassadaga Spiritualist Camp: Box 152, Cassadaga 32706 (904-228-2880).

Dining in the Orlando Area

One of the real pities about Orlando is that far too many of its visitors never take the time to experience its dining scene. Most tend to eat either at the hotels in which they are staying or in nearby fast-food establishments. Until two years or so ago, that was all right because Orlando really didn't have much to offer in the way of gastronomic experience. Since then, however, there's been an explosion of fine new restaurants offering a wide variety of cuisines and styles, as well as comfortable atmospheres. A number of Orlando's new breed of restaurants can easily hold their own against those you would find in some of the nation's major cities.

Granted, it takes considerable devotion to drive perhaps 20 or 30 miles to have dinner after spending a full day at one or more of the area's attractions, but it is worth it. Driving to such northern suburbs as Winter Park, famed for its many fine restaurants, will actually take no more than about 25 minutes. Because things are so spread out in Orlando, locals routinely drive up to an hour to dine in a great spot . . . so there's no reason why you can't do the same.

It's important to remember that while some of Orlando's very finest three-star meals are to be had *in* hotels, the majority are to be found *outside* them. Many of the area's best restaurants never see a tourist, though they've become quite well known and popular with residents.

If you're like most visitors, the meal you are most likely to seek outside your hotel will be dinner. Most Orlando visitors tend to have breakfast in their hotel because it's close, easy, and relatively fast. Lunch, unfortunately, is all too often a matter of grabbing a quick hamburger or slice of pizza at whatever attraction you're spending the day. This is a shame because there are some really fine lunch spots, with lower prices than at dinner. So don't overlook the possibility of taking a longer break for your noontime meal.

At dinner the dress code is usually casual. However, jeans and shorts are almost always frowned upon. A few of the very top-of-the-line restaurants require that gentlemen wear jackets. Ties are never needed, but some older diners sometimes wear them at the more expensive places.

THE TOP THREE

Now that we've pointed out that most of Orlando's very finest restaurants are outside hotels, it's time to point out that the three fanciest, most expensive—but also most fantastic—restaurants are *in* hotels. As luck would have it, two of the three are in the *same* place—the Stouffer Orlando Resort.

Local gourmets and gourmands, along with those from elsewhere, flock to the **Atlantis Restaurant,** a delightfully subdued, romantic, almost "clubby" establishment that dishes up some of the most excellent cuisine you're apt to find anywhere.

You just *know* the place has got class when, as soon as you're seated, a cheerful busboy arrives and fills your glass with Evian water. Waiters, garbed in black tie and tails, are extremely well trained and highly knowledgeable. Most important, they've got the patience to go through and explain to you what is, for Orlando, a rather sophisticated menu.

The Atlantis offers up a wide range of delicate nouvelle cuisine dishes priced from $18.75 to $29.50. A nine-course gourmet "sampler" goes for $48.

The restaurant requires that men wear jackets. Daily dinner hours are 6 P.M. to 11 P.M., and reservations are a good idea, particularly for weekend nights. Call 351-5555 and ask for the concierge if calling during the day, or the restaurant itself if it's 4 P.M. or later. All major credit cards are accepted.

The Wyndham's second sensational restaurant, **Haifeng,** is an operation that is closely and carefully watched over by the talented manager, Meng You, who constantly hovers over the chefs and diners to be sure that everything is being done just right and that guests are enjoying themselves. Mr. You is quite knowledgeable about Chinese cookery, and he'll gladly talk with you about it.

Haifeng is like no Chinese restaurant you've ever sampled. Not only is it extremely refined, but service is unhurried and there's no Column A or Column B. Everything is à la carte, with most dishes prepared in the currently popular Hunan style. The selection of fish or meat entrées ranges in price from about $10.75 to $28 per person. If you've got the time, appetite, and money, you might opt for Haifeng's sensational specialty, the Imperial Dinner for Two.

This culinary high point consists of a cold lamb in soy aspic appetizer; entrée choice of the notorious Mongolian Fire Pot prepared at your tableside with chicken, beef, port, scallops, shrimp, oysters, and assorted Chinese vegetables, Peking duck, slowly roasted until the skin becomes crisp and then sliced extra-thin and served with Mandarin pancakes, or Shanghai Chow Yok, butterflied beef tenderloin with a scrumptious sauce made from a secret recipe brought over from Shanghai; pineapple-fried rice; choice of desserts from a pastry cart;

and teas. The price for this feast is a princely $38 per person.

Haifeng is open from 5:30 P.M. to 11 P.M. nightly. Appropriate attire is required, and reservations are advisable. Book your space in the same manner as for the Atlantis Restaurant. All major credit cards are accepted.

The third entrant in the *troika* of top gourmet restaurants is also the most formal, **Arthur's 27,** where jackets are required but most of the diners, generally an older crowd, wear ties as well.

Situated on the top floor of the Buena Vista Palace Hotel and providing sensational views of the Lake Buena Vista Shopping Village, Epcot Center, and the Magic Kingdom, Arthur's is *the* most expensive place to eat in all of Orlando. Its fixed-price, seven-course Continental super-gourmet dinner costs a hefty $52 per person.

Dinner at Arthur's can be even more pricey than it appears because every single item you order that's not on the set menu is extra . . . a *lot* extra! Wine by the glass, for example, ranges from $4 for a Sterling Vineyards Sauvignon Blanc 1983 to an amazing $55 per glass for Remy Martin Louis XIII Grand Champagne Cognac. American, French, and Italian wines by the bottle range from $14 to $150. Added to everything else is a 16 percent gratuity and five percent tax. Luckily, all major credit cards are accepted.

But if you can afford the price and you like a subtle, elegant, formal kind of place with sensational food, you'll love this restaurant. Arthur's has only 18 tables; in fact, there's only one sitting per night and, as your waiter tells you upon your arrival, "The table is yours for the evening" (which is just as well since the complete dining experience will take a good three hours).

The menu, which is constantly evolving, usually offers eight entrées and six appetizers, all elegantly prepared and served in a rather fussy but colorful and artistic manner.

The restaurant is open daily from 7 P.M. until 10 P.M., but it's best to arrive early to fully savor its delights without having to rush through. The toughest nights to secure reservations, which are mandatory, are Saturday and Sunday, when lots of locals like to come, usually to celebrate some special event. To book, call 827-2727.

More Great Restaurants

While those three may be the most spectacular in Orlando, there are many other fine restaurants in the area.

Many locals and hotel employees are likely to mention a place called **Maison et Jardin** if you ask them to recommend a fine Continental restaurant. Maison, in fact, has become an institution of sorts in Central Florida, though far more residents talk about it than have actually dined there because it too is on the expensive side.

With its lush draperies, sheer curtains, and Roman villa design and decor, Maison et Jardin may sound a bit corny, but it's not; the place is elegant, and the service is impeccable. The quite-extensive menu of excellently prepared dishes features entrées priced from $13.95 to $21, and all major credit cards are accepted.

Jackets are requested. Due to Maison's popularity, it's virtually mandatory that you make a reservation if you hope to dine there. Call 862-4410.

The restaurant is in the northern suburb of Altamonte Springs, at 430 South Wymore Road. To get there, take I-4 East to the State Road 436 exit. Turn left, pass the Expressway and take another left at the first light onto Wymore. Drive about half a mile and you'll see the restaurant's sign on your right.

Dinner is from 6 P.M. until 10 P.M. daily, except Sunday, when it's from 6 P.M. to 9:30 P.M. Locals also flock to Maison et Jardin on Sunday for its celebrated New Orleans Sunday Brunch, served between 11 A.M. and 2 P.M. on the first Sunday of each month. The price for brunch is just $9.95 per person.

DINING IN ORLANDO

Fans of the great (Florida) outdoors love the **Park Plaza Gardens** in suburban Winter Park. This popular restaurant is a see-and-be-seen experience for the locals, particularly the *grand dames* of Winter Park society, the secretaries and suited-up yuppie businesspeople at lunch, and the well-established families of this classy town at dinner.

Because this is an expensive place, with the average dinner costing about $34 per person, the Park Plaza Gardens may make better sense for lunch (though even then it's hardly inexpensive). Luncheon focuses heavily on omelets, quiches, and large salads ranging in price from $6.25 for quiche to $14.50 for lobster salad. Everything is à la carte, with sensational desserts ranging from $3.50 for caramel custard to $10 for baked Alaska or bananas Foster for two. The dinner menu, heavy on seafood, ranges from $14.95 to $21.95 for entrées. All major credit cards are accepted.

Lunch is served Monday through Saturday from 11:30 A.M. to 3 P.M. Dinner is from 6 P.M. until 10 P.M. Sunday through Thursday, and from 6 P.M. to 11 P.M. on Friday and Saturday. On Sunday, there is a very chic Seafood Champagne Brunch a bargain, at $14.95, particularly with unlimited doses of bubbly, mimosas, or Kir Royales.

Park Plaza Gardens, at 319 Park Avenue South, can be reached by taking I-4 East to the Fairbanks Avenue exit. Turn right and continue all the way to Park Avenue, then turn left and go to New England Avenue and you'll see the Park Plaza Hotel. Reservations, particularly for dinner, are strongly suggested. Call 645–2475.

Fans of Italian cuisine know that the food served at **Ristorante LaScala** is among the very best. The restaurant's other highlight is the robust Italian arias courtesy of jovial owner Joseph Del Vento, who is usually moved to sing whenever a customer is celebrating a special occasion.

Though elegant and gourmet style, LaScala is more a neighborhood place than a fancy restaurant, and its popularity led Joseph to expand it in 1985 so that it now seats 150 at tables that are quite close together. Within an hour of opening, virtually every seat is taken, usually by locals who come time and time again. Arrive early, and make a reservation, particularly for weekends, by calling 862–3257.

While loving every item on his full and varied menu, Joseph is particularly proud of his homemade Fettucini Alfredo and will probably do his Jewish-mother act trying to convince you to give it a try. At $9.50, there's more than enough to feed at least two as an appetizer. LaScala's dessert specialty is the Grand Marnier Cheese Cake at $3. A la carte entrées range in price from $10.95 to $21.95 at dinner.

LaScala is open Monday through Saturday from 11:30 A.M. to 2:30 P.M. for lunch, and from 5 P.M. to 10:30 P.M. (11 P.M. on Friday and Saturday) for dinner.

It is located at 205 Lorraine Drive in suburban Altamonte Springs, just north of Winter Park. To get there, take I-4 East to the State Road 436 exit. Take a left and, just after crossing I-4, you'll hit a traffic light at Douglas Avenue. Turn right and drive a few blocks to tiny Lorraine Drive, which will be on your left. LaScala's parking lot is at the corner. It's easy to miss this restaurant, so keep an eye peeled for the Day's Inn, just beyond which is LaScala.

In a town of tradition, Winter Park's famed **Villa Nova Restaurant** has been something of a Central Florida institution for more than 39 years, and justifiably so because it's sensational. Villa Nova, which claims to be the largest freestanding restaurant in Central Florida, is the centerpiece of a three-part, 18,000 square foot building which also houses the popular Cheek-to-Cheek nightclub and showroom on the left side and a lovely 90-seat lounge with live entertainment nightly on the right.

The average check for the Northern Italian cuisine is about $29, with dinner entrées priced from $10.95 to $19.95. Locals also know Villa Nova for its tender and juicy steak dishes. The most popular Italian items at dinner are fettuccine with lobster at $17.95 and the shrimp scampi Lorelei appetizer at $6.75.

Reservations are advised; call 644–2060. Hours are Monday through Saturday from 6 P.M. to midnight for dinner. All major credit cards are accepted.

Villa Nova is at 839 North Orlando Avenue. Take I-4 East to the Lee Road exit, turn left and continue to the intersection with Highway 17–92 (Orlando Avenue). Take a right and watch for the restaurant on your right.

"Neighborhood" French bistros are always a delight to find, especially when on vacation. Orlandoans know just such a place, but tourists rarely ever happen upon **Le Coq au Vin,** and it's a shame because the place is a real find.

Small and nearly always full, this little bistro draws a friendly clientele from yuppies to denim clad couples smooching in a corner.

Le Coq au Vin is owned by Louis Perotte, who runs the kitchen with gusto, and wife Magdalena, the restaurant's charming hostess.

The à la carte dinner menu lists of eight appetizers and 13 entrées. The food is not fancy, but honest and sumptuous, Entrées run from $8.75 to $16, making meals quite a bargain. For a real treat, try the unusual "chicken liver pate Michel". Lunch prices run from $5.50 to $6.50. Major credit cards are accepted.

Le Coq au Vin is open from 11:30 A.M. to 2 P.M. and 5:30 P.M. to 10 P.M. Tuesday through Saturday, and from 5 P.M. to 9 P.M. on Sunday. It's a good idea to call 851–6980 for reservations, especially for dinner.

To get to Le Coq au Vin, which is at 4800 S. Orange Ave., take I-4 east toward the downtown area and exit to U.S. 441 North. Go to Michigan Avenue, turn right, continue to Orange. Le Coq au Vin is just past the intersection with Holden Road.

Indian cookery has been having a difficult time gaining acceptance in Orlando, but those who have tried it at the **Darbar Restaurant** come away raving not only about the wonderful food but also about the magnificent surroundings in which it's served. The name comes from a room in Delhi's famed Red Fort where courtiers went to feast after meeting with the emperor. The restaurant's large, high-ceilinged entrance/reception area is nearly an exact copy of the original Darbar, except for the lavish use of gold and marble, both of which are simulated.

The food is every bit as exciting as the decor, with Tandoori dishes the specialty, though there's also a selection of savory beef, lamb, chicken, and vegetable curries. The best way to get a good idea of the range of fine dishes available at Darbar is to order the Mixed Tandoori Platter, a real treat at $14.95. (This dish is actually enough for two.) Tandoori dishes are priced from $9.95 to $16.95, curries from $6.50 to $10.95. The 10 house specialties range from $11.50 for chicken tikka masala to $16.95 for lobster or whole fish Tandoori.

Darbar is open Monday through Saturday from 6 P.M. to 11 P.M., and from 6 P.M. to 10 P.M. on Sunday. All major credit cards are accepted.

The restaurant is in Orlando's Marketplace shopping center at 7600 Dr. Phillips Boulevard. You usually don't need reservations, though they're not a bad idea if you're going on a Friday or Saturday night. Dress is casual, and the phone number is 345–8128. To get to

Darbar, take I-4 to the Florida Center area and get off at Exit 29, which will put you on Sand Lake Road. Go west on Sand Lake to the second traffic light. When you see the Sun Bank Building, you'll know you're at Dr. Phillips Boulevard. Turn right and enter the Marketplace and you'll see Darbar just opposite the front parking lot.

Despite the nationwide craze for non-beef dishes, America is still heavily populated with people who will do *anything* for a great hunk of steer. **Barney's Steak House** is well known among locals for filling that bill with succulent, top-quality beef that is marinated in apricots. Considering the quality, prices are more than reasonable, with the highest-price steak, a super-fine, nine- to 10-ounce prime filet or T-bone, just $14.95. Chopped steak is just $8.95.

Barney's is open from 5 P.M. to 11 P.M. Monday through Saturday. Reservations are advised if you're going on the busiest nights, Wednesday, Friday, and Saturday, when there often is a line outside. Call 896–6864 to book. All major credit cards are accepted.

To get to Barney's, at 1615 East Colonial Drive in downtown Orlando, take I-4 to the Amelia Avenue exit and continue straight ahead to Colonial Drive. Turn right and continue a couple of miles to Fern Creek Avenue (there's a traffic light). Just past the intersection, you'll spot the restaurant on your left.

Since Florida is surrounded by water on three sides, you would expect the state to be just bursting with thousands of really great seafood restaurants. Unfortunately, that just isn't the case. In fact, it's quite difficult to find a truly good seafood house anywhere in the state, including Orlando. But the popularity of **Bakerstreet Seafood Grille** proves that good quality, a fun atmosphere, excellent service, and the freshest possible product will always draw crowds.

Menu items are extensive but vary depending on the day's catch, fresh from both the Gulf of Mexico and the

Atlantic Ocean, as well as from such distant ocean locales as Boston and Washington State. On a typical evening you're likely to find marinated swordfish for $14.95, American red snapper for $14.95, black grouper for $13.95, or even some dolphin for $12.95. A few items, such as lobster at $20.95, are a bit pricey, but for the most part prices are quite reasonable considering the large size and quality of the portions.

Bakerstreet is usually filled by 8 P.M. each night and virtually empty by about 10 P.M. Between 8 P.M. and 10 P.M., there is often a line outside the door and the wait can be as long as 45 minutes. That's for those who didn't make reservations, so call 644-8811 ahead. Owners will scrupulously honor the reservation, though they will only hold it for 15 minutes past the time you're supposed to arrive.

Hours are Monday through Saturday from 5:30 P.M. to 11 P.M., and Sunday from 5:30 P.M. to 10 P.M. American Express, Visa, and MasterCard are accepted.

Bakerstreet is at 743 Lee Road. Take I-4 East to the Lee Road exit in Winter Park, turn left on Lee and go about three-quarters of a mile. The restaurant will be on your right.

Orlando also has a host of more modest places which, while usually open for dinner, are more ideal for lunch. All are casual and relatively inexpensive.

All lovers of New York- and Miami Beach-style delicatessens should try **Ronnie's,** a long-standing Orlando institution that is the city's answer to the famed Wolfie's in Miami Beach and the Carnegie Deli in New York.

Ronnie's all-purpose menu offers daily hot specials from $3.65 to $7.15, sandwiches from $3.45 to $5, and combination sandwiches from $3.65 to $6.75. Only cash is accepted. A great feature of Ronnie's is its bakery, where you can pick up a variety of mouth-watering breads, cakes, and cookies.

Ronnie's is open from 7 A.M. to 11 P.M., Sunday through Thursday, and from 7 A.M. to 1 A.M. on Friday and Saturday. It is located at 2702 East Colonial Drive, in the Colonial Plaza shopping center. To get there, take I-4 to the downtown area, exit at Amelia Street, and continue straight ahead to Colonial. Turn right and go to the major intersection with Bumby Avenue and you'll see the shopping center on your right. Phone 894–4951 if you get lost.

If there is such a thing as *the* restaurant for the Orlando area cognoscenti, it has to be **Jordan's Grove,** one of the most charming, sophisticated, and delicious experiences in Florida.

It is difficult to decide whether the setting or the food is the more beautiful part of the experience. Jordan's is in one of the area's oldest homes (built in 1912), with delightful views over 3.5 acres of lushly landscaped gardens, fountains, and woods.

The New American dishes change daily, based on availability of fresh ingredients. Everything, even relishes, is homemade. A fixed price of $20 to $30 per person covers a superb four-course dinner; the two-course lunch is $5.50 to $9.50; Sunday brunch is $9.50.

Though Jordan's seats just 65, the owner refuses to turn tables over more than twice during a meal; it takes at least two hours to properly enjoy the artful creations and leisurely service.

Lunch is served Tuesday through Friday from 11:30 A.M. to 2:30 P.M.; dinner is offered Tuesday through Saturday from 6 P.M. to 10 P.M.; Sunday brunch is from 11:30 A.M. to 2:30 P.M. Reservations are strongly advised (628–0020). All major credit cards are accepted.

Jordan's Grove is at 1300 S. Orlando Ave., Maitland. It's easy to miss—watch for the sign to the Enzian Theatre and turn in.

The hearty food and good down-home southern cooking draw both locals and visitors by the carload to International Drive's **O'Scarletts Seafood & Steakhouse Restaurant** for breakfast, lunch, and dinner. Particularly enticing is the special Country Breakfast, a huge bargain at $4.95 for adults and $2.75 for children. At dinner, you can dig into such treats from the Deep South as rib-eye steak, fried catfish, or southern ham steak at prices from $8.25 to $11.25.

Hours are daily from 7:30 A.M. to 11:30 A.M. for breakfast, 11:30 A.M. to 3 P.M. for lunch, and 5 P.M. to midnight for dinner. There are different specials each night and an all-you-can-eat platter priced at $8.95 All major credit cards are accepted.

O'Scarletts is at 6308 International Drive, near Wet 'n Wild, in Florida Center. Phone is 345–0727.

Nightlife in the Orlando Area

For some difficult-to-define reason, most visitors to Orlando—and even some locals—insist that the level of nightlife falls somewhere between meager and nonexistent. The reason for that way of thinking probably lies in the fact that until a few years ago, it was true to a large degree, and people haven't yet caught on to the progress that's been made in recent times. Today the area bustles with all kinds of fun things to do after dark. New places are opening all the time, offering everything from super-sophisticated and flashy discos to relaxed cheek-to-cheek dancing, down-home Country and Western saloons and show-rooms to serious theater and dinner theater, medieval jousting tournaments to comedy clubs.

The place that's most widely known among both tourists and locals is **Church Street Station,** the ultimate, most complete nighttime experience in Orlando. This is the downtown place that almost single-handedly began Orlando's metamorphosis from sleepy town to one offering a tremendous diversity of nightlife for fun-lovers of all ages. It took a lot of daring for owner Bob Snow to open in 1974, since the downtown area was run-down and hardly anybody would venture into it after dark.

NIGHTLIFE *112*

What today is a major, sprawling complex devoted to the good times began with just one feature, Rosie O'Grady's, which today is still its most popular component. As the years passed and Rosie's became more and more successful, the complex kept growing as Snow first acquired the adjoining buildings, then some across the street, all of which he artfully refurbished (and sometimes whimsically decorated) and filled with food, music, shows, and good times. You can pick one specific part of the complex in which to spend an evening or wander, as many do, from area to area, soaking up the individual character of each.

At Church Street Station, a single admission price of $7.95 per person permits you to stay as long as you wish and to do as much as you want, be it dining, drinking, dancing, or people-watching. Food and drink costs are, of course, extra. Parts of the complex are open during the day, mostly for eating, but the place is very quiet then. At night, and particularly on weekends, it can and does get extremely crowded, but that's all part of the spirit of the place, the basic concept of which is to provide good, clean, nonstop fun from early afternoon until the wee hours of the morning.

Rosie's, decorated in 1890s fashion, features Dixieland jazz, with shows daily at 7:30 P.M., 9:30 P.M., and 11:45 P.M. You can get stacked sandwiches and hot dogs in its Gay 90s Sandwich Parlour from 4:30 P.M. to 11 P.M. Apple Annie's Courtyard features continuous live folk and bluegrass music from 8:40 P.M. until 2 A.M., and salads, fresh fruit platters, and specialty drinks from 11 A.M. to 4 P.M. Lili Marlene's Aviator's Pub is strictly for fine dining in an English-pub atmosphere; its primary decorating touch is the large-scale model aircraft suspended from the ceiling. Lili's is open from 11 A.M. to 4 P.M. for lunch, and 5:30 until midnight for dinner. The rock 'n' roll crowd heads for the three dance floors in Phineas Phogg's Balloon Works, open from 7 P.M. to 2 A.M., with breakdance shows Monday, Wednesday, and Friday at 9 P.M., 11 P.M., and 12:30 A.M.; and Tuesday, Thursday, and Saturday at 9 P.M. and 11:30 P.M. Across the street at the beautifully decorated Cheyenne Saloon & Opera House you can partake of excellent barbecue,

Country & Western entertainment and dancing, and shows, sometimes featuring name performers, at 9 P.M., 11 P.M., and 12:45 A.M.

Church Street Station can, at peak evening hours, have as many as 3,000 people packed in, so brace yourself for a lot of noise and action. Besides, that's what makes people love the place. American Express, Visa, and MasterCard are accepted, and dress however you like.

The complex is at 129 West Church Street; its phone number is 422–2434. To get there, take I-4 to the downtown exit at Anderson Street. Continue straight ahead for one block, then follow the signs directly to parking areas. At night, you cannot park on the portion of Church Street housing the complex because it's blocked off to permit easy flow between its various parts and also because it becomes the scene for one of the liveliest block-parties you're likely to see anywhere.

The hottest spot in town right now is another massive place, **J. J. Whispers,** an extremely high-energy, classy, and brassy scene, which, surprisingly, is as popular with those over 30 as with those under that age. J.J.'s tries very hard to maintain an image of class. Many locals who come are dressed in the latest fashions; dress code calls for "tasteful but outrageous" attire.

Admission is $3; more for special concerts. Thursday Ladies' Night provides free admission and 75¢ drinks for women. On Tuesdays between 7:30 P.M. and 10 P.M., women only are permitted in the City Lights Room for male burlesque shows. Various rooms at J.J.'s offer cabaret, comedy, video disco dancing, shows, and late-night snacks with old movies. Hours are Tuesday through Friday from 4:30 P.M. to 2 A.M., Saturday and Sunday from 8 P.M. to 2 A.M.

J. J. Whispers is in the Lee Road Shopping Center. Take I-4 East to the Lee Road exit and turn left. Continue for about half a mile and watch carefully for the sharp left-hand turn at Adanson Street. After the turn you'll see the shopping center. J.J.'s is at the extreme left end of the mall, facing Adanson.

Monday night is usually a very slow time in most towns, but in Orlando there's *always* something going on at **Cheek-to-Cheek,** where Monday night concerts have become one of the area's hottest attractions.

The small club, which adjoins the Villa Nova Restaurant, manages to squeeze in 250 people for the two nightly concerts at tables so close together you'll quickly become best friends with your neighbors. Some really great performances are often given by "name" stars and/or bands in rock, jazz, and country music, who do their thing on a tiny stage over an excellent sound system. Cheek-to-Cheek is usually sold out for both the 8 P.M. and 10:30 P.M. shows; if you can get tickets, you will pay from $10 to $20 per person just to get in, depending on how famous the concert artist or band may be.

Other nights of the week are very popular with the 35- to 50-year-old crowd, who dance to Top 40s music played by Cheek-to-Cheek's house band. Hours are 8 P.M. to 2 A.M., Tuesday through Saturday, and there's a $3 per person cover charge.

To reach Cheek-to-Cheek, which is at 839 North Orlando Avenue (644-2060), take I-4 East to the Lee Road exit. Turn right on Lee and continue to the intersection with U.S. 17-92, which is Orlando Avenue. Turn left and watch for the Villa Nova sign on your right. You can park your own car or use the restaurant's valet.

Locals, tourists, couples, and families all get a big kick out of dinner shows, which offer great food-and-entertainment value plus loads of fun. At this point, you shouldn't be surprised to find that Orlando has an impressive selection of these places as well.

The newest are both in Florida Center, across the street from one another, and are under the same ownership.

King Henry's Feast, at 8984 International Drive, is just what the name implies—a medieval style banquet of five courses, a welcome mead, and unlimited beer, wine, and soft drinks.

There are two dinner-shows; times vary with the season.

Admission is $22.95 for adults, $19.95 for juniors 12–20, and $14.95 for those 3–11.

Just down the street, at 8445 International Drive, in the new Mercado shopping center next to the Orlando Marriott, is **Mardi Gras,** which has, as the name implies, taken for its theme the fun-filled city of New Orleans. Upon entering you're greeted with a mint julep or children's "cocktail," followed by a four-course, sit-down Louisiana dinner of gumbo, salad, entrée choice of chicken or fish, and praline dessert. A New Orleans jazz band works out during dinner, and once you've finished eating, a 90-minute cabaret show with lavish costumes and colorful lighting recreates the Mardi Gras experience. Seatings are nightly at 6 P.M. and 9 P.M. Admission is $22.95 for adults, $19.95 for juniors 12–20, and $14.95 for those 3–11.

You should book in advance for both King Henry's Feast or Mardi Gras; to do so call 351–5151 locally or, from outside the area, 800–641–5151.

You can reach each place by taking I-4 to the Sand Lake Road (State Road 482) exit and proceeding one block to International Drive. Take a right, go just past the Orlando Marriott, and you'll see the Mercado on your left and King Henry's on your right.

Lovers of horses and tales of knighthood should try **Medieval Times,** which also sits inside a "castle". The Medieval era gets quite a different treatment here than it does at King Henry's. The setting is a large, 1,000-seat arena in the center of which knights on horseback joust and generally amuse the crowd while playing out what's supposedly a true story from the Middle Ages. Visitors sit along two sides of the center rectangle and are served a four-course meal that's similar to King Henry's.

Show times are Sunday through Friday at 7 P.M., and Saturday at 6 P.M. and 8:30 P.M. From March through early May, show times are 6 P.M. and 8:30 P.M. on Monday and Thursday through Saturday, and on Sunday at 7 P.M. Admission is $24 for adults and $16 for children 3–12. To book, call 239–0214 from the Orlando area or 396–1518 if you're in Kissimmee.

Medieval Times, which is at 4510 West Vine Street, can be reached by taking the I-4 exit at U.S. 192 East and driving just under seven miles until you see the large castle looming on your right.

Before Disney World, Orlando was a rural, Southern, "red-neck" town, and much of that old spirit remains although the area has undergone tremedous growth and urbanization. With quite a few cowboys left, the area offers many country/western bars, saloons, and lounges.

The most popular, spectacular, and safest of the genre is **Sullivan's Trailways Lounge,** which boasts the largest (1,800-foot) dance floor in Florida. This is a "right-friendly" place where even Yankees are quickly welcomed into the easy-going fold. You will not find urban-cowboy designer jeans here; just the real thing, Stetsons adorn both men and women, who range in age from 21 to over 80.

Admission is $2 Monday, Tuesday, and Thursday; $3 on Wednesday, Friday, and Saturday. Sullivan's hours are lengthy, to say the least—7 A.M. to 2 A.M. daily, except Sunday. Live entertainment begins at 9 P.M. (Country/western "greats" perform in concert here from time to time.)

Sullivan's is at 1108 S. Orange Blossom Trail (U.S. 441). To check who's appearing, call 843-2934.

Index

Adventureland, 65–66
Airport, 12–13
Alfredo di Roma (*rest.*), 78, 81–82
America Gardens Theatre by the Shore, 78
American Adventure, 77, 78
Arthur's 27 (*rest.*), 101–102
Atlantis Restaurant, 99–100
Audio-Animatronics, 62
Au Petit Cafe, 82
Automobile rentals, 15–16

Bakerstreet Seafood Grille (*rest.*), 107–108
Baseball (Circus World), 92
Biergarten (Epcot Center) (*rest.*), 78, 83–84
Big Thunder Mountain Railroad (Magic Kingdom), 66
Bird and the Robot, 75
Bistro de Paris (*rest.*), 82
Bocuse, Paul, 82
Boulangerie Pâtisserie, 79
Buena Vista Golf Course, 51–52, 53
Buena Vista Palace (*hotel*), 29–30
Buses, 15, 19, 22, 56–57

Camping sites, 54–55
Canada, pavilion of, 77, 78
Cassadaga Spiritualist Camp, 2, 97
Central Plaza, 64
Character Breakfasts, 87
Cheek-to-Cheek (nightclub), 114
Chefs de France, Les (*rest.*), 82–83
Children
　admission prices for, 60–61
　Character Breakfasts for, 87
　Hilton facilities for, 28
　restaurant menus for, 79
China, pavilion of, 77–78
　restaurants in, 78
Church Street Station (nightclub), 111–113
Cinderella's Castle, 63
Circus World, 91–92
Climate, 10–11
Clothing, 11–12
Club Lake Villas, 53
Colorado Riders (Circus World), 92
Contemporary Resort (*hotel*), 44, 45, 47–49
　reservations for, 45–46
　Top of the World (*dinner show at*), 86
Coq au Vin (*rest.*), 105–106
Country Bear Jamboree, 66–67
Cross Creek, 2
Cypress Gardens, 92–93

Darbar Restaurant, 106–107
Diamond Horseshoe Revue, 67
Dinner shows, 114–115
Discovery Island, 55, 61
Disney Inn (Golf Resort), 45, 50

Entertainment, 86–87, 111–116
Epcot Center, 1, 42, 71–85
　admission to, 60–61
　Future World in, 73–75
　monorail service for, 56–57
　parking at, 72
　pavilions in, 77–79
　restaurants at, 79–85
　seasons and hours at, 59–60
　tours of, 60–61
　transportation to, 71–72
　World Showcase in, 72–73, 75–76

117

118 INDEX

Epcot Information Center, 74

Fairway Villas, 53
Fantasyland, 68
Ferry, 56, 58
Fishing, 52
Florida Center, hotels and motels at, 19, 34–38
Fort Wilderness Resort Area, 45, 54–55
  Hoop-Dee-Doo Revue at, 87
France, pavilion of, 77, 78
  restaurants in, 79, 82–83
Frontierland, 66–67
Future World, 73–75

Gatorland Zoo, 91
Germany, pavilion of, 77
  restaurant in, 78, 83–84
Golf courses, 25, 31, 44, 51
Golf Resort. *See* Disney Inn
Grand Floridian Beach Resort (*hotel*), 47
Grosvenor Resort (*hotel*), 30
Guided tours, 60–61, 94

Haifeng (*rest.*), 100–101
Hall of Presidents, 68
Haunted Mansion, 67
Hilton Hotel, 28–29
Historic sites, 3, 96
Hoop-Dee-Doo Revue, 87
Hotel Royal Plaza, 30
Hotels and motels, 4, 18–19, 22–38
  Club Lake Villas, 53
  Contemporary Resort, 47–49
  Disney Inn, 50
  Fairway Villas, 53
  in Florida Center, 34–38
  in and near Lake Buena Vista area, 26–32
  Polynesian Village Resort, 49–50
  Resort Villas, 51–54
  top-of-the-line, 22–26
  Treehouse Villas, 54
  in U.S. 192 area, 33–34
  Vacation Villas, 52–53
  at Walt Disney World, 43–49
Hurricane, The (Circus World), 92
Howard Johnson's Resort Hotel, 30–31
Hyatt Regency Hotel, 25–26

I-4 (Interstate highway), 17
Information sources, 6
  at airport, 13
  for Epcot Center, 74
  for Walt Disney World, 62–63
International Drive, 17
Italy, pavilion of, 77
  restaurant in, 78, 81–82

Japan, pavilion of, 77
  restaurant in, 84
J.J. Whispers (nightclub), 113–114
Jordan's Grove (*rest.*), 109
Journey Into Imagination, 74–75
Jungle Cruise, 65

King Henry's Feast (*rest. & nightclub*), 114–115
King Stefan's Banquet Hall (Magic Kingdom) (*rest.*), 70–71
Kitchen Kabaret, 75

Lake Buena Vista, 42
Lake Buena Vista area, hotels at and near, 19, 26–32
Liberty Square, 67
Liberty Square Riverboats, 67
Liberty Tree Tavern (*rest.*), 70
Limousines, 14–15
Living Seas (Epcot Center), 73–74
Lotus Blossom Café, 78

Magic Kingdom, 42, 63–71. *See also* Walt Disney World

INDEX

admission to, 60–61
Adventureland in, 65–66
entering, 64–65
Fantasyland in, 68
Frontierland in, 66–67
Liberty Square in, 67
monorail service for, 56–57
restaurants in, 70–71
seasons and hours at, 59–60
Tomorrowland in, 69–70
tours of, 60–61
transportation to, 63–64
Magnolia Golf Course, 51
Main Street, U.S.A., 64, 67
Maison et Jardin (*rest.*), 102
Major Boulevard, 34–35
Maps, 9
  of Orlando Area hotels, 20–21
  of Walt Disney World, 40–41
Mardi Gras (dinner show), 115
Marrakesh (*rest.*), 84–85
Marriott's Orlando World Center (*hotel*), 22–23, 32–33
Matsu No Ma cocktail lounge, 78–79
Medieval Times (*dinner show*), 115–116
Mexico, pavilion of, 77, 78
  restaurant in, 83
Micanopy, 95–96
Mitsukoshi (*rest.*), 84
Monorail, 43, 56–57
Morocco, pavilion of, 77
  restaurant at, 84–85
Morse Gallery, 2
Motels. *See* Hotels and motels
Motor launches, 56, 58

Nightlife, 3–4, 111–116
  in Walt Disney World, 86–87
Nine Dragons Restaurant, 78
Norway, pavilion of, 77

Orange County Civic/Convention Center, 35
L'Originale Alfredo di Roma Ristorante, 78, 81–82
Orlando, 1–8
  climate of, 10–11
  history of, 7
  hotels and motels in, 4
  information sources for, 6
  map of, 9
  nightlife in, 111–116
  restaurants in, 3, 98–110
  sightseeing in, 94
Orlando area hotels, map of, 20–21
Orlando International Airport, 12–13
O'Scarletts Seafood & Steakhouse Restaurant, 109–110

Palm Course (golf), 51
Parking
  for Epcot Center, 72
  for Magic Kingdom, 64
  for Walt Disney World, 58–59
  for Walt Disney World, hotel guests, 46
Park Plaza Gardens (*rest.*), 103
Park Suite (*hotel*), 36–37
Passports, for Walt Disney World, 60–61
Pavilions, 77–79
  restaurants in, 79–85
Peabody Orlando (*hotel*), 35–36
Peter Pan's Flight, 68
Pickett Suite Resort (*hotel*), 30–31
Pirates of the Caribbean, 66
Plaza Restaurant, 70
Pleasure Island (*rest., shopping & nightlife complex*), 47
Polynesian Village Resort, 43, 45, 49–50
  Polynesian Revue at, 86–87

INDEX

Radisson Inn Maingate, 33
Rawlings, Marjorie Kinnan, 2, 96
Reception Center, 52
Rentals
 of cars, 15–16
 of trailers, 55
Reservations
 for hotels in Walt Disney World, 45–46
 for nightclubs in Walt Disney World, 86–87
 for restaurants at Epcot Center, 74, 80–81
Resort Villas, 45, 51–54
Restaurants, 3
 at Buena Vista Palace, 29–30
 at Contemporary Resort, 48
 dinner shows, 114–115
 at Epcot Center, 79–85
 at Hilton, 28
 at Hyatt Regency Hotel, 25–26
 at Magic Kingdom, 70–71
 nightclubs, 86–87
 in Orlando area, 98–110
 at Stouffer Orlando Resort, 24
Rides
 in Adventureland, 65–66
 in Circus World, 91–92
 in Fantasyland, 68
 in Frontierland, 66–67
 in Future World, 73–75
 in Liberty Square, 67
 in Tomorrowland, 69–70
 in Wet 'n Wild, 89–90
Ristorante La Scala, 104
River Country, 54–55, 61
Ronnie's (*rest.*), 108–109
Rose & Crown Pub, 79, 85
Rosie O'Grady's (*nightclub*), 112–113

San Angel Inn (*rest.*), 83
Sea World of Florida, 88–89
Sheraton Lakeside Inn, 33–34

Sightseeing
 outside Walt Disney World, 88–97
Sonesta Village Hotel, 37–38
Spacecoast Parkway (U.S. 192), 33
Space Mountain, 65, 69–70
Spaceship Earth, 73–74
Stouffer Orlando Resort (*hotel*), 23–24
 restaurants in, 24
Sullivan's Trailways Lounge (*nightclub*), 116
Swiss Family Island Tree House, 66

Taxis and limousines, 14–15
Tennis, 25, 31
Tickets, 60–61
Tomorrowland, 69–70
Top of the World (*rest.*), 48
 dinner show at, 86
Tours, 60–61, 94
Town Square, 64
Town Square Café, 70, 71
Trailers and trailer sites, 54–55
Transportation
 to Epcot Center, 71–72
 within Epcot Center, 76
 between hotels and Walt Disney World, 19, 22
 to Magic Kingdom, 63–64
 within Orlando, 14–15
 to Orlando, via air, 12–13
 from Resort Villas, 52
 within Walt Disney World, 43, 55–59
Transportation Ticket Center (TTC), 56
Treehouse Villas, 54
Tropical Serenade, 66
20,000 Leagues Under the Sea (Magic Kingdom), 68

INDEX

Typhoon Lagoon (*water-entertainment center*), 47

U.S. Highway 192, hotels and motels on, 19, 33–34
United Kingdom, pavilion of, 77
 restaurant in, 79, 85
Universe of Energy, 75

Vacation Villas, 52–53
Villa Nova (*rest.*), 104–105
Viscount Hotel, 30–31
Vistana Resort (*hotel*), 31–32

Walt Disney World, 1–2, 39–43. *See also* Epcot Center; Magic Kingdom
 Club Lake Villas in, 53
 Contemporary Resort (*hotel*), 44, 45, 47–49
 Disney Inn in, 50
 entertainment at, 86–87
 Fairway Villas in, 53
 Fort Wilderness Resort Area in, 54–55
 golf in, 51
 hotels in, 43–49
 hotels and motels near, 19
 information for, 62–63
 Lake Buena Vista hotels and, 26–32
 lines at, 8
 maps of, 40–41
 Polynesian Village Resort in, 49–50
 Resort Villas in, 51–54
 seasons at, 59–60
 tours of, 60–61
 transportation within, 55–59
 Treehouse Villas in, 54
 Vacation Villas in, 52–53
 Walt Disney World Central Reservations Office, 27
Walt Disney World Railroad, 64
Walt Disney World Shopping Village, 52
WEDway PeopleMover, 69
Wee Links at the Disney Inn (golf course), 51
Wet 'n Wild, 35, 89–90
Wilson World Maingate, (*hotel*), 34
Wineries, 95
Winter Park, 2
World Showcase, 72–73, 75–76
 lagoon at, 72–73
 pavilions in, 77–79
 restaurants in, 79–85

Zoomerang (Circus World), 92

FODOR'S TRAVEL GUIDES

Here is a complete list of Fodor's Travel Guides, available in current editions; most are also available in a British edition published by Hodder & Stoughton.

U.S. GUIDES

Alaska
American Cities (Great Travel Values)
Arizona including the Grand Canyon
Atlantic City & the New Jersey Shore
Boston
California
Cape Cod & the Islands of Martha's Vineyard & Nantucket
Carolinas & the Georgia Coast
Chesapeake
Chicago
Colorado
Dallas/Fort Worth
Disney World & the Orlando Area (Fun in)
Far West
Florida
Forth Worth (see Dallas)
Galveston (see Houston)
Georgia (see Carolinas)
Grand Canyon (see Arizona)
Greater Miami & the Gold Coast
Hawaii
Hawaii (Great Travel Values)
Houston & Galveston
I-10: California to Florida
I-55: Chicago to New Orleans
I-75: Michigan to Florida
I-80: San Francisco to New York
I-95: Maine to Miami
Jamestown (see Williamsburg)
Las Vegas including Reno & Lake Tahoe (Fun in)
Los Angeles & Nearby Attractions
Martha's Vineyard (see Cape Cod)
Maui (Fun in)
Nantucket (see Cape Cod)
New England
New Jersey (see Atlantic City)
New Mexico
New Orleans
New Orleans (Fun in)
New York City
New York City (Fun in)
New York State
Orlando (see Disney World)
Pacific North Coast
Philadelphia
Reno (see Las Vegas)
Rockies
San Diego & Nearby Attractions
San Francisco (Fun in)
San Francisco plus Marin County & the Wine Country
The South
Texas
U.S.A.
Virgin Islands (U.S. & British)
Virginia
Waikiki (Fun in)
Washington, D.C.
Williamsburg, Jamestown & Yorktown

FOREIGN GUIDES

Acapulco (see Mexico City)
Acapulco (Fun in)
Amsterdam
Australia, New Zealand & the South Pacific
Austria
The Bahamas
The Bahamas (Fun in)
Barbados (Fun in)
Beijing, Guangzhou & Shanghai
Belgium & Luxembourg
Bermuda
Brazil
Britain (Great Travel Values)
Canada
Canada (Great Travel Values)
Canada's Maritime Provinces plus Newfoundland & Labrador
Cancún, Cozumel, Mérida & the Yucatán
Caribbean
Caribbean (Great Travel Values)
Central America
Copenhagen (see Stockholm)
Cozumel (see Cancún)
Eastern Europe
Egypt
Europe
Europe (Budget)
France
France (Great Travel Values)
Germany: East & West
Germany (Great Travel Values)
Great Britain
Greece
Guangzhou (see Beijing)
Helsinki (see Stockholm)
Holland
Hong Kong & Macau
Hungary
India, Nepal & Sri Lanka
Ireland
Israel
Italy
Italy (Great Travel Values)
Jamaica (Fun in)
Japan
Japan (Great Travel Values)
Jordan & the Holy Land
Kenya
Korea
Labrador (see Canada's Maritime Provinces)
Lisbon
Loire Valley
London
London (Fun in)
London (Great Travel Values)
Luxembourg (see Belgium)
Macau (see Hong Kong)
Madrid
Mazatlan (see Mexico's Baja)
Mexico
Mexico (Great Travel Values)
Mexico City & Acapulco
Mexico's Baja & Puerto Vallarta, Mazatlan, Manzanillo, Copper Canyon
Montreal (Fun in)
Munich
Nepal (see India)
New Zealand
Newfoundland (see Canada's Maritime Provinces)
1936 . . . on the Continent
North Africa
Oslo (see Stockholm)
Paris
Paris (Fun in)
People's Republic of China
Portugal
Province of Quebec
Puerto Vallarta (see Mexico's Baja)
Reykjavik (see Stockholm)
Rio (Fun in)
The Riviera (Fun on)
Rome
St. Martin/St. Maarten (Fun in)
Scandinavia
Scotland
Shanghai (see Beijing)
Singapore
South America
South Pacific
Southeast Asia
Soviet Union
Spain
Spain (Great Travel Values)
Sri Lanka (see India)
Stockholm, Copenhagen, Oslo, Helsinki & Reykjavik
Sweden
Switzerland
Sydney
Tokyo
Toronto
Turkey
Vienna
Yucatán (see Cancún)
Yugoslavia

SPECIAL-INTEREST GUIDES

Bed & Breakfast Guide: North America
Royalty Watching
Selected Hotels of Europe
Selected Resorts and Hotels of the U.S.
Ski Resorts of North America
Views to Dine by around the World

AVAILABLE AT YOUR LOCAL BOOKSTORE OR WRITE TO FODOR'S TRAVEL PUBLICATIONS, INC., 201 EAST 50th STREET, NEW YORK, NY 10022.